Placing Shadows
Lighting Techniques for Video Production

Third Edition

Placing Shadows
Lighting Techniques for Video Production
Third Edition

Chuck Gloman
Tom LeTourneau

Focal Press

AMSTERDAM • BOSTON • HEIDELBERG • LONDON
NEW YORK • OXFORD • PARIS • SAN DIEGO
SAN FRANCISCO • SINGAPORE • SYDNEY • TOKYO

Focal Press is an imprint of Elsevier

Focal Press is an imprint of Elsevier
200 Wheeler Road, Burlington, MA 01803, USA
Linacre House, Jordan Hill, Oxford OX2 2DP, UK

∞ Recognizing the importance of preserving what has been written, Elsevier prints its books on acid-free paper whenever possible.

British Library of Cataloguing-in-Publication Data
A catalogue record for this book is available from the British Library.

Library of Congress Cataloging-in-Publication Data

Gloman, Chuck B.
  Placing shadows : lighting techniques for video production / Chuck Gloman, Tom LeTourneau. — 3rd ed.
    p. cm.
Includes bibliographical references and index.
ISBN-13: 978–0–240–80661–7   ISBN-10: 0–240–80661–1
1. Video recording—Lighting. I. LeTourneau, Tom. II. Title.
TR891.G56 2004
778.59'2—dc22   2004061989

ISBN-13: 978–0–240–80661–7
ISBN-10: 0–240–80661–1

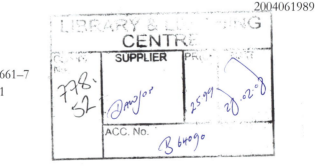
Printed in China
10 9 8 7 6 5 4 3 2

Contents

This third edition is dedicated to my mentors at Penn State University: Bill Urricchio, Steve Fenwick, Jerry Holway, and Rich Curilla—all talented individuals who helped shape what I am today—someone who is still trying to figure out what he wants to do for a living.

Introduction

The subtitle of this lighting text is *Lighting Techniques for Video Production*. It is based on the premise that you place your key and fill instruments in positions that produce the most effective shadow patterns. Shadow patterns are created in order to establish mood and location, provide concealment, establish flattering portraiture, accentuate texture and create interesting composition.

Most people confuse the term "illumination" with "lighting." However, a scene may be illuminated, yet far from lit. You will understand the distinction before reaching the last chapter.

Now then, what else can you expect from this book? You can expect to be more aware of the tricks and equipment used by the professionals. When you have finished reading, you will not be an expert lighting designer; that will not happen until you light many sets under a variety of trying circumstances. However, learning about the special accessories and methods I am about to describe will make your work easier and your results more professional. Lighting isn't an illusion, it is reality. When you erect a light, I guarantee you will get illumination—it may not be the exact effect you desire, but you will see light. The first step is to have a purpose or reason for this particular light.

If you were raised as I was, you believe that federal marshals will storm your home and arrest you for removing the tag from new pillows. After all, the ominous warning reads, "Do not remove under penalty of law." Well, I have come to the point in life where I rip them off and cry, "Come and get me."

I was also raised to believe it is a crime to write in books. But I am going to request that you throw caution to the wind and write in this one. Trust me. Your mother will not punish you, and I need your cooperation in order to make an important point about the intentions and methods of this text. Let's try this "writing in a book" test.

In Diagram 1 (page viii) you will find a jumble of numbers. Get a pencil and give yourself 30 seconds to draw a continuous line from number 1 to number 2 to number 3, etc. At the end of 30 seconds stop and make a note of the number you last connected to the series. Got everything you need? Pencil poised? (The truly brave may use a pen or Sharpie™.) Stop watch set? OK! Ready . . . begin.

How did you do? Now we will see if we can improve your score. In Diagram 2 (page x) you will see the same jumble of numbers. Notice that there are four small dots located around the edge of the jumble on this page. Draw a vertical line from the dot in the center at the top to the dot in the center at the bottom of the jumble. Now draw a horizontal line connecting the two dots on the left and right sides of the jumble.

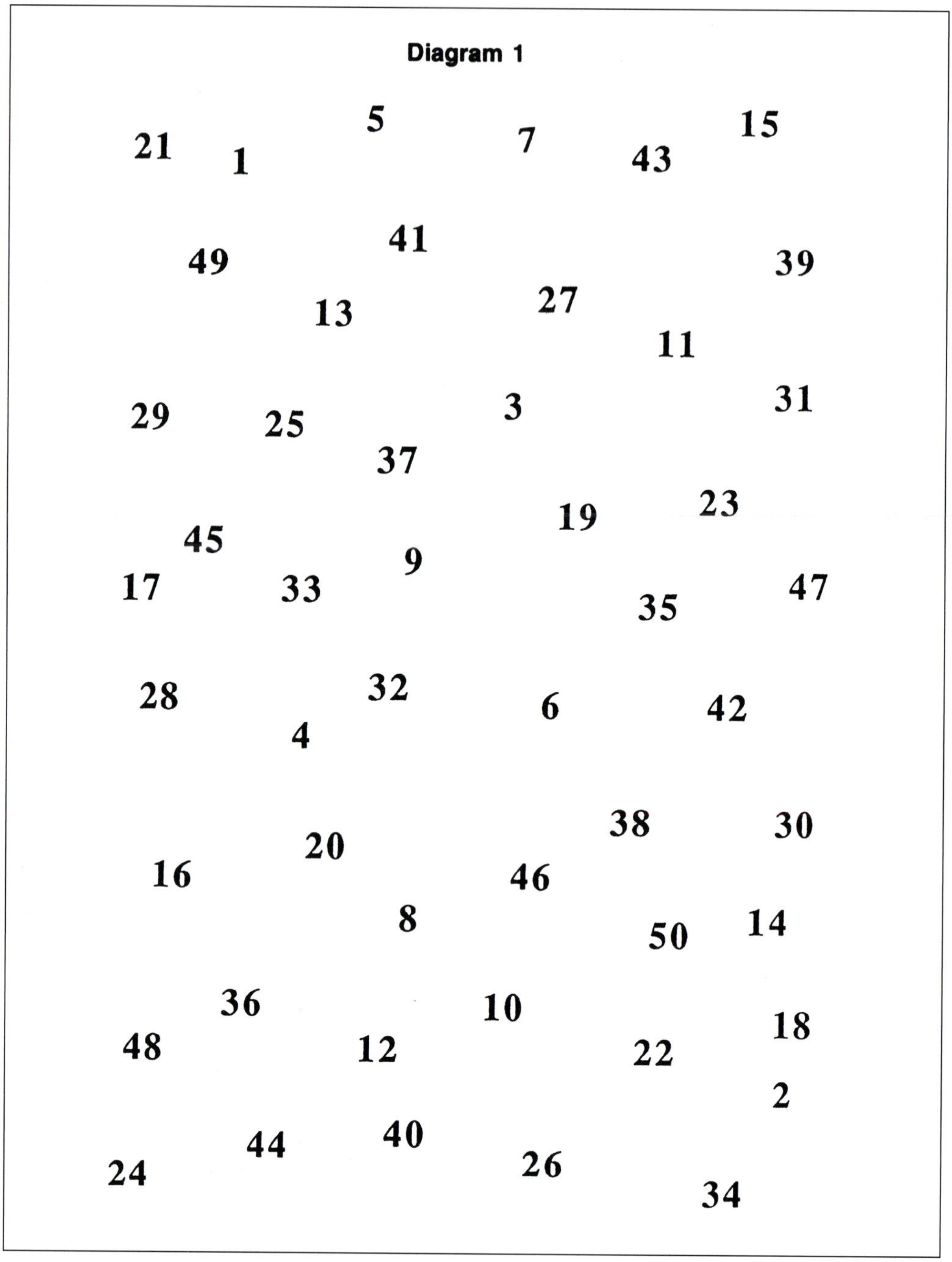

Diagram 1

21 1 5 7 43 15

49 41 39

13 27

11

29 25 3 31

37

19 23

45 9

17 33 35 47

28 32 6 42

4

38 30

16 20 46

8 50 14

36 10

48 12 22 18

2

44 40 26

24 34

Now the jumble is divided into quadrants. Starting at the top left quadrant of the jumble, write number 1. Put number 2 at the top right corner, number 3 at the bottom right corner, and number 4 at the bottom left corner.

I'll also point out that the numbers are arranged so that the first numeral in a series of four numbers is found in the first quadrant. The next number is located in the third quadrant. The following number will be in the second quadrant, and the next in the series will be located in the fourth quadrant. Then the pattern starts over again. In order, the numbers are found first in quadrant 1, then in quadrants 3 and 2 and finally in quadrant 4. Got it? Good! Now give yourself another 30 seconds and try again.

Armed with that new information you reached a much higher number this second time around, I am sure. While there has been no improvement in your IQ, there has been quite an improvement in your ability to complete the specific task.

In a way, that is what this book will do for your lighting skills. It will not improve your IQ, but it will make it easier and more enjoyable for you to light sets. The book is designed to encourage you to go out and try new things—to experiment and to be creative. After all, like the producers of The Outer Limits, you have total control over what the viewers see and how they perceive it.

A lone lighting instrument is a pretty poor lighting tool. This is especially true of the open-faced instruments that are commonly used for location lighting. The creative control of light is the result of using the various accessories available. You will read about many of them, look at photos of them, and learn the roles they play in the control of light. Some uses will be suggested for each item, but do not limit yourself to the examples given. Try other applications and experiment. Controlling the placement of shadows and spill is what good lighting is all about, so there is a heavy accent on the use of accessories. You may already know about some of these; others may be completely new to you. Some are nice to have, others are a must.

You must light to accommodate the limited capabilities of an electronic system. It is essential that you understand how that system reacts to light; you must also know a bit about the physical properties of light itself. I am the first to admit that I am not an electronics expert or a physicist, and you do not need to be one either to acquire a basic understanding of these disciplines as they relate to your work with lights. Before you learned some inside information about the number jumble earlier, you wasted time looking all around for your next selection. You are just as likely to waste time lighting a set without some inside information about the properties of light and the way the television system is designed to react to those properties. You will make a series of uninformed decisions about instrument selection and placement. Often you may be working against your intended goals.

I begin with some painless lessons in physics and electronics. Every effort has been made to keep explanations non-technical, so hopefully I will understand them. A clear understanding of the first

Diagram 2

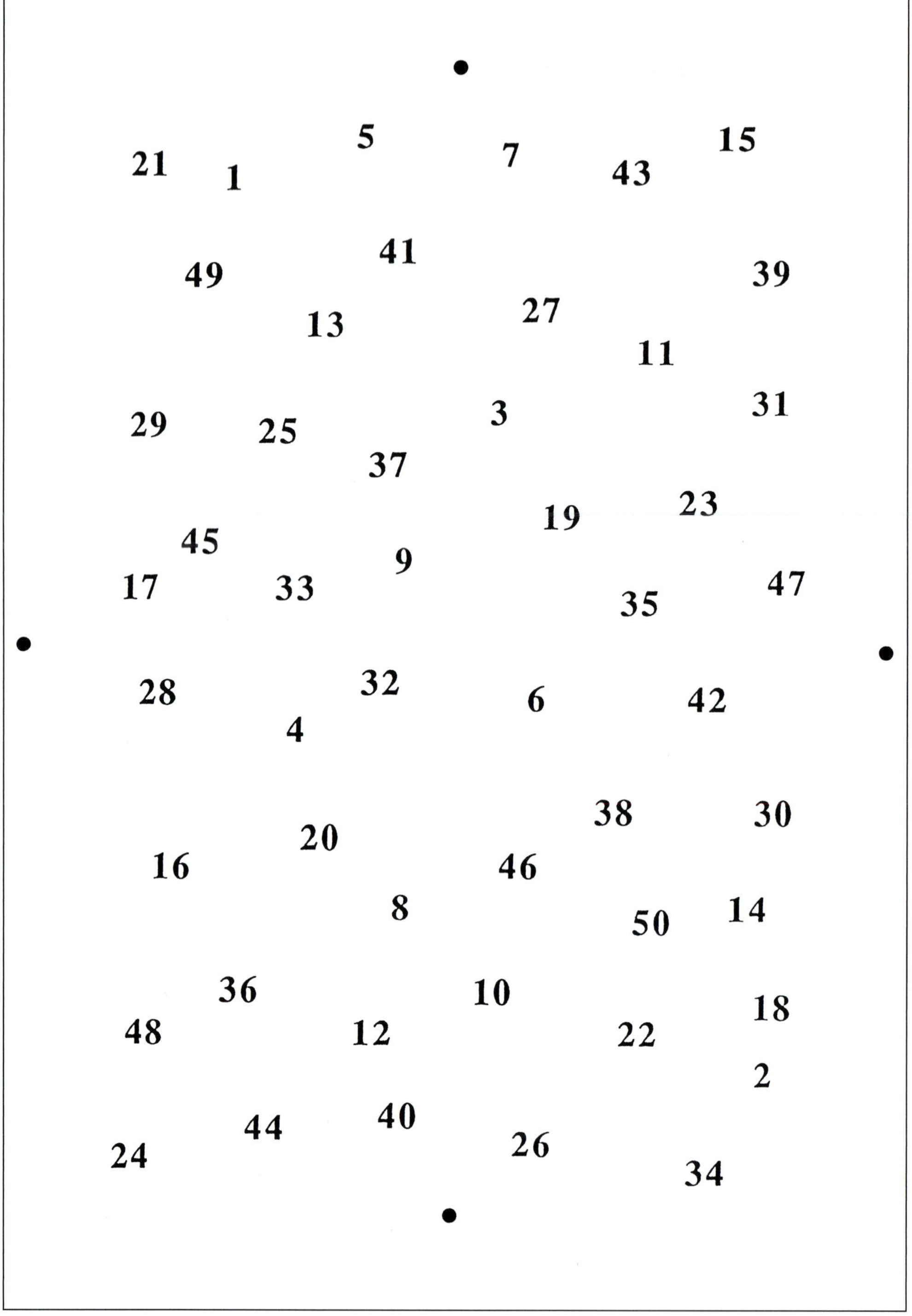

•

21   5   7   15
  1   43
                     43

  49   41   39

      13   27
              11

29   3   31
  25
      37

          19   23
  45   9
17   33   47
          35

•   •

  28   32   6   42
     4

          38   30
   20
16   46
  8   50   14

  36   10
48   12   22   18
                  2

  44   40
24   26
          34

•

x

three chapters is essential groundwork for the remainder of the text. There are many authoritative books that deal in greater detail with the subjects of the first three chapters; they are listed in the Recommended Readings at the end of the book. So read on, enjoy, and experiment. And learn to view the art of lighting as an opportunity to create and to make a great contribution to each scene. Remember, viewers can see only what you let them see. Your task is to place the correct amount of light where it is needed and to keep it off areas where it is a distraction. You should provide no more, no less.

I do not believe it is possible for any book to teach you how to light every conceivable situation; every lighting setup is different from every other one. What this book will do is provide the facts necessary for you to make informed decisions regarding instrument selection and placement to meet the challenges faced on location. You will learn to analyze a scene in terms of how lighting can assist with mood, indicate time, and control space. You will learn to analyze and emulate nature, to make the best use of existing light. You will learn to be a watt miser and to use fewer instruments and accessories to light a scene. You will learn to control and create shadows that enhance and clarify the intention of a scene. In other words, you will learn the art of lighting.

Acknowledgments

I would like to thank the following people: Jerry Holway, my film instructor at the Pennsylvania State University, who was the first to teach me lighting; Bill Urricchio, Ph.D., who would show me the principles and techniques that existed in films; Richard Curilla, my mentor at Penn State University, who gave me the chance to prove my skills in the real world and taught me invaluable lessons; Kathy D'Alessandro, Ph.D., my film director and friend throughout graduate school; Steve Fenwick, Ph.D., who persuaded me to continue on and get my Masters Degree; Charles Samu of Home Box Office, who bought my Masters student film "*The Butler Did It*" and got me started "on my way"; Steve Schreuder, who acted in most of my student films and was patient enough to let me learn, and who co-produced and funded my films before college; George Winchell, from whom I learned a great deal of new techniques with available lighting equipment; Greg Ressetar, who helped hone my lighting talents with a dose of levity; Tom Landis, whose insights and creativity stretched me to the limits; Todd Taylor, whose directorial skills and handling of talent has taught me volumes; Mike Gorga of Megcomm Productions, who I have known since the beginning and who still has "the passion" for this business and keeps it infectious; Brian McKernan, past Editor of *Videography*, who gave me a shot and published my first magazine article; Traci Sibalic, Managing Editor of *TV Technology*, who gave me my first lighting column; Mark Foley, past Editor of *Videography*, who enjoyed my warped sense of humor enough to publish my articles; Mark Pescatore, PhD, Editor of *Government Video*, for giving me my first monthly column on video product reviews; my parents, for believing in me throughout the slow process of figuring out what I wanted to do with my life; and my wife Linda, for letting me do what I needed to do to make a mark in this business.

My students have been an extremely valuable resource because their minds are open to new concepts. Seeing the realization on their faces when they learn what lighting can do is incredible. You may already be a teacher (anyone who explains the craft to others is a teacher and it doesn't have to be in a classroom). If you aren't now, you will become one shortly because that's how you increase your knowledge.

Some people on the set may have done this too long and are tiring of the whole process. Distance yourself from those individuals and hang around with those who still have the passion. For me it's still George, Greg, Tom, Mike, and Todd. Without beating this subject to death—learn the basics and go out and try it for yourself.

And most of all I would like to thank God for giving me the talents and abilities to do what I enjoy best. Some people never find what they are good at. I was fortunate.

Chuck B. Gloman

Preface to the 3rd Edition

This book has been updated with the following items added:

- Information on newly designed lighting instruments (i.e. LED lights)
- Expanded sections on HMI and Fluorescent lighting
- A chapter on how to light specific scenarios with exercises for students to duplicate the set-up in addition to come up with their own lighting plan using the same instruments as well as different ones
- Lighter and smaller lighting instruments and how to use them effectively
- Color images throughout

As the title of this book implies (*Placing Shadows: Lighting Techniques for Video Production*), when you illuminate a set or location, your desire is to have a purpose for each shadow and where it falls. In other words, you are "placing shadows" exactly where you yearn for them to be (or not to be, that is the question).

When I first started in this illustrious field back in 1978, my idea of lighting was to erect a 1000 watt open faced light or 300 watt photo flood in a scoop and immediately start shooting. Luckily that was a long time ago and I've learned a bit more over time. Through time, watching others, and experience, you learn that there is much more than setting up a light and being satisfied that the set is now "lit."

Knowing where and why each shadow is placed on your set or location puts you in control. Since we are the ones with the brains, we should decide where an inanimate object like a light is going to reside on a set and what we desire it most to do. Although this book may not be a beginner's guide to lighting, it will stress the initial concepts of the art, and by using the tools of the trade, achieve the success (in lighting) that you are after.

It is my goal that this book will be your guide to help you better understand and appreciate all that film and video lighting can actually do.

I've been told that lighting is the hardest thing to do in film or video production. This isn't true. I guess it is difficult to set up a light, plug it in, and turn on the switch. The easy part is positioning the instrument, silking or gelling it, and generally making it do exactly what you want it to do. You are only limited by your imagination.

My belief is that you learn best by doing. You can gain understanding and knowledge from this book, taking courses, and learning from others in the field—but until you actually set up the light and see what it does yourself, the picture isn't complete. Read and learn what each lighting unit can do, what happens if you raise or lower it, put it at an angle, diffuse or gel it? After this reading and learning phase, take the light and see if what you learned is true in your application.

My strength in college and film school was the camera. I was able to frame shots well and hand-hold a camera steadier than most—I was extremely fortunate.

However, the main role of a cinematographer or DP (director of photography) is to create the illusion for the camera to record. Part of that illusion is lighting. Since my main focus (pardon the pun) was camera work, I had to learn a new skill: lighting. By practicing, experimenting, and just doing it, I was able to learn which end of the light not to look into. Throughout the rest of film school and graduate school I was asked to light and shoot every-one's student films. Most of the other students aspired to be directors, but I wanted to shoot. We all got what we wanted.

Once out of college I was faced with two dilemmas: the real world and videotape. The techniques of lighting video aren't any different than film. The cameras and editing equipment have changed totally, but the same lighting concepts apply to both. I don't want to underemphasize the importance of practicing and experimenting. I've learned a great deal from others by watching (not copying) what they did. I could have easily taken a picture of their setup and duplicated it on my set. Like cheating, that would have accomplished nothing. I want to know why the lights are set up a specific way.

A friend of mine copied another colleague's lighting setup down to the extension cord. When he finished with the duplicated setup, the client didn't like it. He said, "Change it." If my friend would have just learned the technique the original party used, he would have saved a lot of setup time. The clients are always right (except when they're wrong), and if they don't like your setup, you'd better be willing to change it. They will be paying the bill, and you are working for them. That's why it is so important to learn your craft and not just blindly "do it."

More light doesn't mean a better lighting setup. Some people can work wonders with three lights, others need an arsenal. Some have also said, "Oh, if I just had a 10K, then I'd be able to light the scene." You might be able to light it brighter with a 10K, but you better know what you're doing. Although large lights offer more illumination, they aren't better lights. These "big boys" were designed for a specific purpose—lighting large areas—and they do it well. If the director wants sun streaming in through the windows, these units are the sun. If he later wants a soft shaft of moonlight to fall on the leading lady, the 10K would have to be strongly diffused or the talent would be charred.

Through common sense and a little experience, you will learn what each lighting instrument does best.

If your lights are the paints, then your light meter is the brush. Instead of throwing the paint all over the place so it covers everything, use your brush to put light only where it's needed and looks best. This technique separates the artist from the painter.

This book won't have all the answers, but hopefully it will help you generate more questions. Through experimentation (after learning the concepts) your skills will grow. You never stop learning, and if you ever do—you're dead. This book has been a great learning experience for me. Some of the solutions to the problems I encountered while on the set may help you in your specific situation.

Surround yourself with talented people in the art of lighting like I did. Some of it is bound to rub off on you. I've learned from lighting masters that I've been fortunate enough to work with: George Winchell, Greg Ressetar, Tom Landis, Mike Gorga, Tom Mooney, and countless others. I even interviewed one of the greatest living masters of lighting and cinematography: Director of Photography Vittorio Storaro A.S.C., A.I.C. He has always inspired me and his work is untouched by others. "The details are in the . . ." I would like to complete that famous quote by adding only one word—lighting."

Never allow yourself to say on a set in reference to lighting, "It can't be done." Nothing is impossible. It might be extremely difficult to do what you want with the equipment you have, but it is never "impossible." This is where experimentation comes into play again. Pull from the knowledge you do have and tackle the problem from that angle. I've worked with people who know all the terms and concepts and say, "what you are trying to do won't work." Don't believe them until you try it. It may only take a few minutes and after you've seen for yourself, they may be right. But you need to see and prove that first before you just blindly accept that. Along that same lines, if I tell you something is so—don't take that as gospel. I make mistakes, have typos, but to the best of my knowledge, the concept has worked for me. Try it yourself and see if I am smoking kitty litter.

In writing for trade magazines like *Videography* and *Government Video*, I write about only what I've learned from a specific situation. This is the situation, this is how I attempted to light it, and this is what happened. Sometimes I was fortunate enough to come up with something better.

I would like to take this opportunity to thank Steven Bradford, Media Arts Chair at Collins College in Tempe, Arizona for reviewing my manuscript for this book, pointing out areas that needed improvement, and offering suggestions on how to make it better. This took a lot of his valuable time and I appreciate his effort. Thank you!

Chapter 1
The Physics of Light
Starting on the Right Wavelength

Light is a particular range of electromagnetic radiation that stimulates the optic receptors in the eye and makes it possible to determine the color and form of our surroundings.

Light has three properties that contribute to our perception of the things it illuminates:

- color
- quality
- intensity

Lighting directors must have a basic understanding of all three properties, from a scientific point of view, to make an artistic contribution to the productions they are lighting. In Chapter 1, we will deal with the aspects of color and quality; in Chapter 3, we will discuss the quality of light provided by various lamp and reflector types; and in Chapter 4, we will discuss aspects of intensity.

Color

We know that the light of the sun or of an electric lamp can be broken down into the colors of the rainbow. The common method for dispersing white light is by using a prism. As a young science student you may have learned the memory crutch Roy G. Biv to help you remember the colors and the order they fall in when white light passes through a prism and is projected on a white surface.

Primary Colors

Light has two components: luminance information and chrominance information. The luminance information deals with the amount of light intensity in lumens and is measured in foot-candles. Chrominance (color) information is subdivided into two factors: hue or tint, and saturation.

Hue defines color with respect to its placement within the spectral range, as shown in Figure 1.1. It is the basic color of the light. The term "tint" is often used interchangeably with hue in defining chrominance and in labeling the monitor control that adjusts that aspect of color.

Saturation is the property of light that determines the difference from white at a given hue. In other words, heavily saturated red might be described as fire-engine red. A poorly saturated red is closer to white in value and may be called pale pink. Unfortunately, most monitors just label the saturation control as color.

To understand saturation, think of color as a specific hue that gradually increases in intensity along a straight line from white at the left end to the pure color on the right. The pure color—for example, red—is said to be saturated, while its unsaturated hue is called pink. Adjusting the color control of a monitor or television affects the degree of color saturation in the scene.

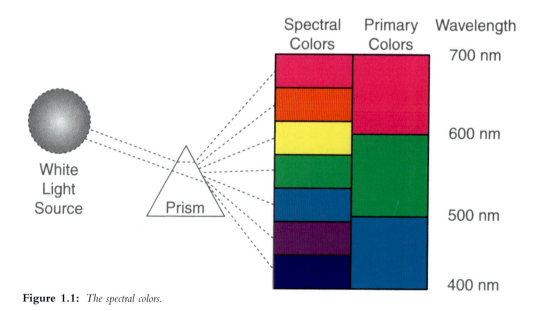

Figure 1.1: *The spectral colors.*

Figure 1.1 shows that white light consists of at least seven distinct colors, known as the spectral colors. We know from observation that there are a great many other colors in the world around us. In the great scheme of things, these seven colors are of no particular importance except to illustrate the concept of refraction and that white light has distinct component parts—parts that can be measured. There are three primary colors, however, that are extremely important in understanding the physics of light and the transmission of color pictures by the television system. These colors, the capital letters of the name Roy G. Biv, are red, green, and blue. They are the primary colors of light. Various combinations of these three colors make it possible to reproduce all the other colors in the visible spectrum. Since this is true, we need only evaluate everything we see in terms of how much red, green, and blue light it reflects to reproduce its actual color. That is why the television camera has three pickup chips, each one reacting to the percentage of a particular primary color reflected by the subject. The display screen, a cathode ray tube (CRT), contains red, green, and blue phosphors that glow with an intensity relative to the signal generated by the corresponding pickup chips in the camera.

While the knowledge that white light could be broken down into seven colors in a particular order may have gotten us through our science test, we need to understand the color aspects of light in greater detail to understand how it affects the television camera (see Figure 1.2). Red has the longest wavelength of visible light. The farther you proceed toward the violet, or opposite, end of the spectrum, the shorter the wavelengths become. People commonly use the term "warm" to identify light in the red-orange portion of the spectrum and "cool" to describe light in the blue-violet end of it. These terms are subjective evaluations that relate to the perceived or psychological effect of these colors on the viewer. These terms should not be confused with the objective measurement of the actual spectral composition of a light source known as the "color temperature."

Color Temperature

The color temperature of a light source is determined by the wavelengths of light it emits. That is, how much red light, how much green light, how much blue light, etc. We know that as an object is heated it will first glow with a reddish color. If we continue to apply heat, it will give off a yellow light and change to blue and then violet as additional heat is applied. Because different substances emit different wavelengths of light when heated to identical temperatures due to their differing chemical compositions, a specific substance must be used to establish standards.

Such a standard is called a "blackbody." This mythical body, or substance, is said to be composed of a material that neither emits nor reflects any light whatsoever. When it is heated to a specific temperature, it gives off a specific combination of wavelengths that are consistent and predictable. The temperature scale used is Kelvin (K), in which 273° Celsius is absolute zero. In theory, when we heat this body to a temperature of 3200°K, it will emit a certain combination of wavelengths through the yellow end of the spectrum. It is classified as "white light" because it contains sufficient wavelengths of all the colors of the visible spectrum which, when added together, form

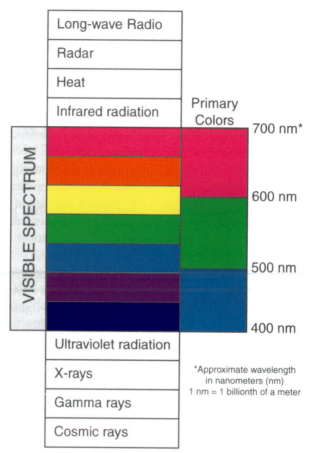

Figure 1.2: *Electromagnetic spectrum and approximate wavelengths in nanometers.*

white. If we continue heating the body to a temperature of 5600°K, it will emit additional wavelengths nearer the violet end of the spectrum.

The important part of this definition is that the light emitted during the heating process progresses at a gradually increasing rate from the longer red wavelengths to the shorter wavelengths in the blue–violet end of the spectrum. This phenomenon occurs only when a tungsten filament is heated by passing a current through it. Incandescent lamps produce this gradual, predictable increase when current is applied to their filament.

For reasons both scientific and economic, tungsten is the metal of choice for manufacturers of lamp filaments. Since the melting point of tungsten is 3800°K, a working temperature of 3200°K has been chosen as the standard for tungsten lighting. At an operating temperature of 3200°K, a tungsten filament will have a relatively long life span and still produce a desirable spectrum. The tungsten lamps designed to burn at 3400°K for special photographic applications have greatly reduced life spans due to higher operating temperatures. The closer you operate a filament to its boiling point, the shorter its life.

Some tungsten–halogen lamps are rated at 5600°K, or "daylight." Since the filament will vaporize at 3800°K, how can a color temperature of 5600°K be achieved? The answer is the application of dichroic filters. These are special optical coatings applied to the front of daylight lamps that reduce the colors complementary to blue and produce a pseudo-daylight spectrum. Most daylight sources, like the halogen metal iodine (HMI) lamps, are the result of specially designed discharge lamps that generate the higher color temperature without the need for special dichroic coatings that reduce output and lamp efficiency. No true blackbody source can produce the daylight spectrum, since no metal filament can be heated to 5600°K or higher, without melting.

Fluorescent lamps, on the other hand, do not produce light as the result of passing current through a filament. Instead, an arc of current passes through a combination of gases, excites them and causes a phosphor coating inside the lamp to glow. Such light sources do not produce a continuous spectrum and are very difficult to correct and balance with standard light sources. Sometimes you may see a correlated color temperature listed for some fluorescent lamps. Generally, such a listing will rate a cool white lamp at 4200°K and a warm white fluorescent lamp at 2900°K. Do not be misled by such ratings, however. They are not really scientific and do not provide satisfactory results when you add filters based on those temperatures to such a source. It merely means that a certain number of people have looked at this light source and agreed that it appears to the human eye to produce a blackbody color temperature that correlates with 2900°K or 4200°K. It is not actually 2900°K or 4200°K. *No light sources, other than incandescent lamps, are true blackbody sources, measurable in degrees Kelvin.*

Fluorescent lights, mercury vapor lamps, sodium vapor lamps, and various other multivapor discharge sources all produce a very erratic spectrum and cannot be rated in degrees Kelvin as blackbody sources can. The actual wavelengths produced depend on the composition of gases and the coatings on the interior of the lamps. The spectrum they produce does not provide a true white light containing known wavelengths from the red end of the spectrum to the violet end. Since they do not produce a true white light, they are very difficult to color-correct with filtration media (see the section later on in this chapter, "Working with Sources of Mixed Color Temperature").

Color Rendering Index

A more scientific approach to the classification of the apparent color temperature of fluorescent and other discharge lamps is recommended by the International Commission of Illumination. That method is the color rendering index (CRI), in which eight standard pastel colors are viewed under the light source being rated and under a blackbody source of known color temperature. The color rendering index ranges from below zero to 100. A number on that scale is assigned to the rated source light based on how accurately it renders the pastel colors compared to the same swatches viewed under the blackbody source. The closer they come to matching the look of samples under the blackbody source, the higher the index number assigned to the source being tested. Cool white fluorescent lamps are given a CRI of 68. Warm white fluorescent lamps have a CRI of 56. Daylight (Daylite) fluorescent lamps have a CRI of 75. A special fluorescent lamp called the Vita-lite has a CRI of 91 and comes as close as possible to a natural or daylight source.

Light radiates from the source in waves. The length of these waves, when measured from peak to peak, varies with the color involved. As mentioned earlier, the longer wavelengths are near the red end of the spectrum. These are perceived as being warm in color. The shorter wavelengths, near the violet end of the spectrum, are perceived as being cool in color.

While the human eye is capable of adapting to a wide range of color temperatures and interpreting color correctly, the pickup chips of the television camera cannot. Television cameras are designed to produce accurate color when the scene is illuminated with light at 3200°K. Within a given range the camera circuits can compensate for slight deviation from the ideal 3200°K color temperature (see the next section, "Auto White Balance"). This color temperature is often referred to as "tungsten" light. The other general color temperature classification is "daylight." It ranges anywhere from 5400°K to 6800°K. These color temperatures are usually found when shooting in sunlight or under specially balanced or color-corrected studio lights.

Camera Operation

Before plunging into a technical explanation of camera operation or, later on, proper setup techniques for a color monitor, let me say a word about why such topics are covered in a text about lighting.

To make valid judgments about your lighting efforts, you must be able to view the results through the system. A number of texts dealing with TV lighting state that your monitor should be properly adjusted before you can make a valid assessment of the scene. They do not, however, tell you how to adjust it properly. Understanding proper adjustment methods is important for both the independent video producer who must know some basic aspects of lighting and for lighting designers who work with monitors daily.

In Figure 1.3, we see that the light that passes through the lens is split up by the prism block by a charged coupled device (CCD) into three primary colors. Each CCD chip then produces a voltage signal that is relative to the amount of that particular color present in the image at any given location. For example, if we were shooting a primary red art card, the red chip would produce the entire signal, and the green and blue chips would produce no signal at all.

According to the National Television Systems Committee (NTSC) standards for American television, the camera should be set up to produce a 1-volt signal, from peak to peak, when it is properly adjusted. In the case of shooting the red art card mentioned earlier, that entire signal would

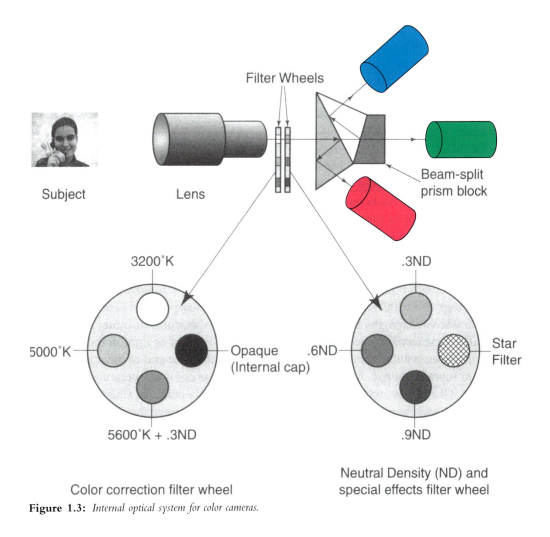

Figure 1.3: *Internal optical system for color cameras.*

be produced by the red chip. However, we rarely shoot a subject that contains a single primary color, so all pictures will be composed of varying voltages from each of the three CCD chips. Since white contains all the colors of the visible spectrum, we can reason that if we reproduce white accurately, we will automatically reproduce individual colors accurately. When white is reproduced on television there is a definite ratio among the three primary colors. In that ratio, red is 30% of the total signal, blue is 11%, and green is 59%.

Auto White Balance

To achieve the ratio for proper reproduction of white, and subsequently colors, the modern camera is designed with auto white balance circuits. These circuits are able to make adjustments in the output voltages of the three CCD chips so that their combined outputs form a 1-volt signal from filter out the blue-violet wavelengths that are in excess of those found in 3200°K light sources. Typically, they will be rated around 5000°K and 6500°K.

Some manufacturers assume that when the 6500°K filter is necessary, the scene will be so bright that you have to stop down to your smallest f-stop. For this reason, they combine the 6500°K setting with a 0.3 neutral density (ND) filter to reduce your depth of field somewhat. ND filters are designed to equally reduce the amount of light in the red, blue, and green spectrum. They do not affect the color temperature. A 0.3 ND filter reduces light by 1 stop. It is a nice touch, but it generally does not provide adequate control over your depth of field. For greater control, you should have a set of ND filters that can be placed in front of your lens to cut back the incoming light. The normal complement of such a filter pack is 0.3ND, 0.6ND, and 0.9ND, which reduces the light by 1, 2, and 3 stops, respectively. The filters may be used in any combination to give even greater latitude of control. They permit you to work with larger f-stops so not everything is in focus from 3 feet in front of the camera to the horizon. [Two sources for screw-on ND filters are Belden Communications, Inc. and Tiffen (see the Appendix). They also make a variety of other effects filters that will be discussed later.]

A few older studio cameras have two filter wheels, like the one illustrated in Figure 1.3. One wheel is for color correction filters only and one wheel for a complete set of ND filters and pos-

Figure 1.5: *An example of a camera white balanced for daylight using tungsten instruments as a lighting source. Note the orange cast.*

Figure 1.6: A: *An example of a camera white balanced for tungsten lighting outdoors. Note the blue cast.*
B: *An example of a camera white balanced for tungsten lighting under fluorescent lighting. Note the green cast.*

Figure 1.11: *Gelling a window on the inside.*

Other than warming the gaffer tape, use light stands and attach the tape to them instead of the buildings exterior. Use your ingenuity and you'll come up with a solution (or avoid shooting and lighting in cold weather).

Failure to convert all of the light sources in any scene to a common temperature will cause expensive and sometimes impossible color-correction problems in the post-production phase. Never take the attitude, "I'll fix it in post." In many cases you cannot fix it, and when you can, it is usually very time consuming. You may end up either chewing up your time in the editing room or paying someone else to do it. Do it right the first time—when you are lighting. One hour of color correction on the NLE system will just about buy that gel material.

New Products to Solve Lighting Problems

One of the most encouraging developments in lighting during the recent years is the application of space-age technology to produce products that will solve these and other problems faced by the lighting designer. Experiments have been progressing with special coatings on the interiors of multidischarge lamps and fluorescent tubes to produce a spectrum that can be color corrected to standard photographic temperatures. Special reflectors have been developed that absorb ultraviolet and infrared radiation. Lamp and reflector designs are being perfected to fit in smaller, more efficient instruments, and lamp spectrums are becoming more compatible with CCD chips. There are now more durable and accurate filtration and reflector materials available as the result of new plastics and dyes.

Fluorescents presented a substantial problem. Though they were developed back in 1867 by Becquerel, they did not appear on the consumer scene until the 1940s. Even then they did not receive wide acceptance. One of the first wide uses was in supermarkets because of their need to light large areas evenly. Store owners complained to lamp manufacturers that fluorescents made the meat look blue, and that oranges and other produce looked bad. As a result, the tubes were redesigned to correct these problems. Had the first complaints come from a cinematographer rather than a butcher, we probably would not be cursed with the strange spectrums these lighting sticks produce today. These instruments are now commonplace on news sets and many other video shoots. We'll go into much greater detail on fluorescents later.

Solving the Problems of Mixed Color Temperature

Let's analyze that interview scene where the talent is seated in front of an undraped office window and the office is lit by fluorescents. We will achieve satisfactory results using some "inside" information about a variety of readily available accessories.

Since the primary rule of good lighting is that all the sources must be the same color temperature, you have to decide which temperature you want to make standard. Will you color-correct the daylight and fluorescents to match your 3200°K sources, or will you convert your studio lamps to daylight and leave the fluorescents alone, or correct them to daylight also?

You can do any of these things by using the correct color-correction media, and you must do something to bring all your light sources to the same color temperature.

If the window is behind the talent, and we will put it there for purposes of illustration, it may not be a wise decision to leave the window alone and place booster blue correction filters on your 3200°K lamps to convert their color temperature to daylight. While you can satisfy the criteria of matching the color temperature of sources this way, you will still be left with an impossible contrast problem. In all probability, if you expose for the window, the talent will end up in silhouette because your lighting kit will not be powerful enough to overcome the strong backlight. If you expose for the talent, you will "blow" the window. It will become a screaming white blob behind the talent. The excessive white level will not be handled by the white clipping circuits of your camera, and you will experience breakup on playback.

Your problem will be aggravated by the fact that you will also lose efficiency when you convert from tungsten to daylight by placing a booster blue filter in front of the source. If you require a full blue to convert 3200°K to a nominal 5500°K daylight, you will reduce your light output by 64%. The transmission of full daylight blue is 36%. If you can get by with half blue to convert 3200°K to 4100°K daylight, you will reduce your light output by only 48%. The transmission of half blue is 52%.

The easiest thing to do would be to close the drapes or pull the shade on the window, but you may want to see out the window to help establish location. You can accomplish this goal by placing a sheet of ND material on the inside of the window. This polyester-based material comes in rolls 100 feet long by 48 inches wide. It is optically clear, does not affect color temperature, and can be reused many times if properly cared for. Static cling will usually be strong enough to hold the sheet in place on a small window. Larger sheets can be taped in position.

Once you have reduced the incoming light sufficiently, you can set up your front lighting in the normal manner using booster blues in front of each studio lamp. As with the ND filters you screw on the front of your lens, ND sheets come in 0.3ND, 0.6ND, and 0.9ND to reduce the light source by 1, 2, or 3 stops.

If there are other windows in the room, off camera, their light can serve as general fill or can be bounced into dark areas of the scene with a reflector without any color correction. The natural light will cut down on the amount of color-corrected incandescent light you need to add to the scene.

Filter material commonly known as 85 converts daylight sources to 3200°K. Some 85 is combined with 0.3ND, 0.6ND, or 0.9ND filtration material to reduce daylight and change its color temperature in one operation. If you choose to correct daylight to tungsten so you can work directly with your 3200°K sources, it would be necessary to gel the off-camera windows or cover them so they would not add daylight to the scene. Obviously, it is better to be able to use the additional window light without having to color correct it.

The term "gel" is used here as a verb. Gel was the original material to which dyes were added for the purpose of coloring light sources in the theater. A solution of liquid gel, with dye added, was poured into large pans and permitted to solidify into thin sheets. It is still used as an economical alternative to modern plastic filtration material in low-wattage theatrical instruments, but it will not withstand the higher temperatures of quartz-halogen lamps. Gel is frequently used as a verb to describe the act of placing color-correction or ND material in the color frame of an instrument or on the surface of a window.

The fluorescent lights could be left alone if you use daylight as your standard. Their color temperature will blend in rather well with daylight. Or you can convert them to daylight by using a Minus-green filter. Fluorescents can also be converted to 3200°K by using a Fluorofilter filter in front of the tubes. You can place a color-correction sheet above the plastic lens or grid of the fluorescent fixture, or, if the tubes are exposed, you can purchase sleeves of filter material that slip right over the lamps. If you find yourself shooting repeatedly in the same office location, you may wish to leave your sleeves or sheets in the fixtures to save time on your next setup. A drawback to this approach is that the Fluorofilter reduces the light output by 64%. Its transmission is only 36%.

You can purchase fluorescent lamps rated at tungsten or daylight temperatures for installation in areas frequently lit by fluorescents. These lamps are more expensive than regular fluorescent tubes but they may be worth it if you shoot often in a given office area that is lit by fluorescents. If you are working on a tight budget, it may be possible to transfer the cost for these lamps to building maintenance. This would give you a threefold gain: there is no cost to your department to re-lamp the fixtures, you get a 3200°K source to work with, and you also save time by not having to gel the fixtures the next time you shoot in that area.

The Spectra 32 fluorescent tube from Luxor Lighting Corporation (see the Appendix) is rated at 3200°K and given an 82 on the CRI scale. The Luxor Vita-lite fluorescent is rated at 5600°K and given a 91 on the CRI scale. Such lamps are the best choice for lighting in a makeup room because they provide excellent color rendition of subtle makeup shading. Their color temperature will match the light sources on the set and they will not add heat to the makeup area. Do not use a string of household lamps around your makeup mirrors. Their color temperature makes critical evaluation impossible and their heat becomes uncomfortable as the actors work close to the mirror.

How Filters Work

The issue of using color-correction filters to correct for the strange spectrums of discharge lamps and fluorescents seems to be shrouded in an aura of mystery. While having lunch one day, two lighting designers were asked by an expert in the area of color correction, "What do you do to correct for fluorescents on location?" They looked at each other and one replied, "We start drinking early."

Second case: The author of an excellent and very thorough text on filmmaking offers a scientific explanation of filtration formulas. In summing up things and trying to explain the reasons for selecting certain filters, he states, "Don't try to figure it out; it's like a game and those are the rules."

The issue also seems to be made overly complicated. After numerous conversations with leading experts in the design and manufacture of filter materials, I find confusion of terms how to explain how filters work. It is not uncommon to talk of booster blues and imply, if not state outright, that they add blue light to the tungsten spectrum to balance it with daylight temperatures that contain more blue. That sounds fine. It even looks fine. If we view a light source that has been gelled with booster blue, there is a definitely bluer tint to the light that passes through it.

A pamphlet that is no longer in print, describing light control media, stated, "There are gels to add enough green to daylight sources to match fluorescent phosphors permitting an overall correction with a single lens filter."

If the drinking water at your house has a funny taste, you buy a filter for your faucet and it makes the water taste better. Does it add good taste to the water that passes through it? No. It removes the chemicals that cause bad taste. That is all filters can do–remove things, whether they are objectionable chemicals in a water supply or objectionable frequencies of light. Why then do the experts talk of adding green or boosting blues? Actually, the people who make such statements are not the physicists and chemists who formulate these filters and who know such statements to be false. The problems are caused by copywriters and salespeople who try to simplify the technical aspects of their products. The result is greater confusion on the part of the users who are not better informed, but misinformed.

The Rosco Cinegel pamphlet is an excellent resource to have. It illustrates products currently available to control color temperature, and to reduce intensity and products that reflect light sources. The pamphlet is available free from Rosco (see the Appendix). It presents an overview of their products and gives practical application examples. You should also send for their swatch book that contains samples of booster blue, reflection media, light control Media, diffusion media, and daylight control media. Once you are familiar with these products, you will see that someone has already invented material to solve many of the problems you face daily in interior and exterior location lighting and in studio setups. Lack of knowledge about these and other helpful products available to the professional will cause you to come home with compromised video. There is no need to settle for unsatisfactory lighting, because the tools exist to correct the problems you face.

Think back to our efforts to fool the camera during white balance so that it would produce a warmer look. We did not add red to the picture. We balanced on a cyan chip. In effect, we were removing a color complementary to the red, namely cyan, to create the appearance of more red in the picture. The same is true of color-correction filters. They cannot add green as the text of the pamphlet stated, but they can remove magenta, which is the complement of green. That will produce an apparent increase of green in the light that passes through them.

Look again at the faceplate of the vectorscope in Figure 1.8. You will see that green is at 241° on the scale. Its complement, magenta, is 180° opposite that point at 61°. When we remove the magenta, the light appears greener because its complement is lacking. Light that passes through ND material is dimmer, not because the filter adds black but because it subtracts equal amounts of the red, blue, and green light. Filters can shift emphasis by removing complements of problem frequencies when they are present. They can also remove the offending frequency directly, if it is present in the spectrum at levels in excess of those needed to conform to the desired color temperature.

When a source, like the sodium vapor lamp, produces a wildly erratic output with many holes in the normally continuous spectrum of a blackbody source, filters are not able to compensate for the missing components. If you filter out the offending frequency, you create even larger holes in

Table 1.1: *Commonly Encountered Light Sources
and Their Approximate Color Temperatures*

Source	Color Temperature (°K)
Candle flame	1900
Sunlight—sunrise or sunset	2000
100-watt household lamp	2865
500-watt household lamp	2960
1000-watt household lamp	2990
Quart-halogen studio lamp	3200
Photoflood and reflector flood lamps	3400
Sunlight—early morning	4300
Sunlight—late afternoon	4300
Daylight blue photoflood	4800
Carbon arc	5000
Sun arc lamp	5500
HMI lamp	5600
Direct midsummer sunlight	5800
Overcast sky	6000
Summer sunlight plus blue sky	6500
Skylight	12,000–20,000

the spectrum and generate new problems for yourself. Since frequencies that complement the offending spikes do not exist, you cannot filter them out to shift the apparent output of the source. In short, completely effective color correction is a physical impossibility. Some color correction is possible, but do not consider yourself a failure when the colors are not perfect under such adverse lighting sources. Keep in mind that even the human eye does not perceive colors accurately under such lights and the viewer does not expect to see natural colors in such locations (see Table 1.1).

Quality of Light

It is possible to measure the color temperature and the intensity of light with the proper meters. I will discuss the aspect of intensity later, but for now I would like to deal with the third characteristic of light which plays a very important role in the aesthetic look or "feel" of the scene. That characteristic is the quality of the light. Quality can be judged by the density and sharpness of cast shadows. Granted it is a subjective evaluation, but on one end of our scale we have harsh specular sources that cast dense shadows with sharp, well-defined edges. The highlights are specular and the contrast range is high. On the other end of the scale we have soft diffuse sources that cast transparent shadows with poorly defined out-of-focus edges. The highlights are softened and the overall contrast range is lower.

The quality of the light accounts for the different look of two outdoor scenes. One take is shot on a heavily overcast day. The other is shot at the same location on a bright, sunny day. Despite proper exposure and color balance, the two scenes will look very different because of the quality of the light at the time of shooting.

As a lighting designer, you should not only be concerned with putting the right amount of light in the right places, but you should also evaluate and control the quality of the light you use. Fortunately, there is a battery of filtration products available to allow you to do just that. There are accessories to precisely control the quality of studio light and to change the basic quality of exterior light. These diffusion materials will be discussed later in the text.

The majority of lamps used today generate light when an electrical current is passed through a thin tungsten filament. The filament heats up as a result of its resistance to the flow of electrons. The heated filament emits photons of light that radiate in all directions from many points along its surface. One of light's unique properties is that it does not require a medium in which to travel from place to place. Sound and heat cannot travel through a vacuum, but light can. Sound and heat are slowed down by travel through liquids, but light is not.

The harshest form of light is known as "point source illumination," where all of the energy emanates from a single point and travels outward in a series of straight lines like spokes radiating from the hub of a wheel (see Figure 1.12). These straight rays cast crisp, well-defined shadows. There are no criss-crossed rays to soften the edge of cast shadows. This is the type of light present on a bright, cloudless day, like the one described in the previous example. The only artificial light sources that produce near-point-source illumination are the carbon arc and the HMI lamp.

Since the majority of lighting instruments use some configuration of a tungsten filament enclosed in a glass or quartz envelope, we will take a look at what happens to the light rays that are produced by such multipoint filaments. If we pick only one point along the filament to illustrate the properties of light, we can study the effects that lamp construction have on the visible spectrum (see Figure 1.13).

The ray that passes most directly from the filament to the atmosphere outside the envelope is an example of efficient transmission.

In the process of that transmission the ray is refracted, or bent, as it passes through the envelope to the outside air. Light will be bent whenever it travels from one medium to another of a

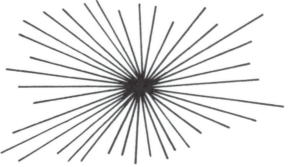

Figure 1.12: *A radiating light source.*

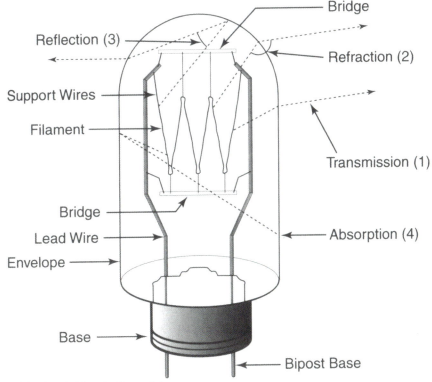

Figure 1.13: *A typical lamp's effect on light rays.*

different density. The same behavior can be observed in Figure 1.1, which shows light passing through a prism.

The next ray we observe does not pass directly through the envelope. It is *reflected* (3) from the interior surface one or more times before transmission occurs.

A fourth ray does not escape the envelope at all. It is an example of *absorption* (4). The absorbed ray is converted to heat energy by the envelope. The four characteristics of light shown in this figure are emanating from a single point along the filament. The fact that these behaviors are occurring at an infinite number of points along the filament in a random sequence produces a quality of light that is much less specular than that produced by single point sources. The random aspect of the transmitted rays can be altered and reshaped by the lamp housing, internal reflector and lens system of the instrument.

Lamp Output

While the electric light has been a great boon, a modern-day consumer advocate might argue that it is a device promoted and sold by utility companies to take unfair advantage of the public,

lesson to be learned is that you should place instruments as far from subjects as possible to eliminate severe falloff problems.

You should understand that by moving the source farther from the subject you will be decreasing the overall light level by a factor that is inversely proportional to the square of the distance. However, that reduced level will be more evenly distributed over the subject. In Figure 1.13, there was no difference in the meter readings because the sun is so far away that falloff is not measurable over reasonable distance changes. If you were to take a meter reading on the top of a very tall building and at ground level, there would be no measurable difference between the two readings because of the extreme distance between the sun and the relatively close distances between the two readings on earth.

When working in homes and offices with low ceilings, there is a tendency to place the camera and lights close to the subjects to lessen the lighted area and reduce power requirements. This becomes problematical when there is any movement by the subjects. If they stand, their heads suddenly seem to fluoresce while their lower bodies are underexposed. Raising the instrument as high as possible and moving it back as far as possible will help even out the great differences in intensity between seated and standing subjects.

Figure 1.17: *Scrims and flags in front of a light source.*

Figure 1.18: *Diffusion material in front of light sources.*

Once you have done what you can to let physics reduce the effects of falloff by moving the light as far from the subject as possible, you must turn to accessories to complete the elimination of the problem. There are three different things you can do to even out the light on a subject that moves closer to, or farther from, the light source during a scene.

The simplest solution, if your instrument is equipped with an accessory shoe, is to place a graduated scrim in it and turn the scrim so it reduces the light at the top of the beam. Graduated scrims are invaluable tools and come in many degrees and configurations. You can achieve the same effect using an ordinary window screen in a gel frame holder, and the shape of the reduced intensity area can be tailored to specific situations. Another quick fix is to place a section of ND filter in the top portion of a gel frame and insert it in the accessory shoe.

The third solution involves a little more hardware, but the philosophy is the same: Reduce the light output in the upper portion of the lighted area. If you are using an instrument without an accessory shoe, you can mount scrims, nets or ND material on a separate stand and place them in front of the source. This method actually offers the greatest control. The greater the distance between the source and the diffusion material, the more pronounced the transition will be. Examples of this method can be seen in Figure 1.17 and Figure 1.18.

A graduated scrim can be turned to reduce the lower half of the light beam from a key light to keep excess foot-candles off a white suit coat and still provide enough light on the face of a dark-skinned subject.

The rate of falloff differs from instrument to instrument depending on the make and type. Falloff from softlights and floods is greater than falloff from spots because of the diffuse nature of their rays, which dissipate more rapidly. Specular sources fall off less rapidly because their rays are parallel.

The hard part is over. If you have understood all of the information in this first chapter, the remainder of the text will be as easy as burning your fingers on a barn door.

Chapter 2
Meters, Monitors, and Scopes
Looks Good Here!

One of the common wisecracks in television is, "Looks good here!" It is uttered by someone who is claiming that the signal is fine at that end, and if there is a problem, it must be the fault of the person at the other end of the line. That "other end" may be down the hall from the studio in the tape room or it may be across the country after several microwave links, fiber optic runs, and a satellite hop. Regardless of how complex the ultimate link is, the fact remains that the original signal must be technically correct.

Meters

The light meter and the color temperature meter are the only tools available with which to predict the final outcome of cinematographers' or videographers' lighting efforts. They combine those tools with their experience to form judgments about exposure and color temperature correction. In most cases, that is enough to get the job done, and good cinematographers will rarely mess up. However, in film, they can never be completely sure of their exposures until they view the processed film. Video is more forgiving because most cameras have color viewfinders or flip-out LCD screens which enable immediate results. Studio cameras are still tethered to monitors, and someone at that end must determine if it looks "alright."

Light Meters

To maintain proper lighting ratios and exposure ratios it is necessary to use a light meter calibrated in foot-candles. There are two kinds of light cells used in meters today: (1) selenium cells and (2) cadmium sulfide (CDS) cells. Selenium cells generate a current that is proportional to the amount of light falling on them. The CDS cell modulates the current provided by a battery in a manner directly proportional to the amount of light reaching the CDS.

Even though CDS meters are more sensitive than selenium cell meters, their added sensitivity is of no value to you if you are shooting in areas that are extremely dark, simply because it will be too dark to make good pictures under such adverse conditions. In dark environments, even though the "lux" illumination may be as low as a dark environment, the video grain increases with the absence of lights.

That added sensitivity helps the photographer who can shoot under all types of natural lighting conditions with extremely fast film. In video, the "gain" must be increased to achieve a properly exposed image. Increased gain means increased grain and noise.

Other qualities dealing with ruggedness and ease of use make CDS meters a good choice for the videographer. Selenium light cells and the CDS type of cell are used in meters of two general types.

Reflected Light Meters

The auto iris system in the television camera is really a form of a reflected meter. It reads the total light reflected by the subject and adjusts the iris so that the camera does not produce a signal strength greater than a preset value, usually 100 IEEE units. IEEE (pronounced "eye triple E") stands for the Institute of Electrical and Electronics Engineers.

If you are my age, you may still refer to the IEEE as the IRE (Institute of Radio Engineers), but it has merged with the AIEE (American Institute of Electrical Engineers) and changed its name. The IEEE scale on the waveform monitor (WFM) ranges from −40 IEEE units to 140 IEEE units. As a point of reference, −40 IEEE units = 0.3 volts and 140 IEEE units = 1.0 volt.

Like a camera's auto iris system, the handheld reflective meter measures the total light reflected by the scene. It is aimed at the scene from the camera position and the reading is taken, producing an average reading for the scene. If you are more concerned about specific areas, such as the flesh tones of an actor, you can walk close to the subject and point the meter at the actor's face with your back to the camera. A warning about the obvious: Be sure not to cast a shadow on the subject when you take your close reading.

Spot meters are a specialized form of reflective meters (see Figure 2.1). They measure a narrow angle of the total scene, usually 1°. They have a built-in reflex viewing system so that you can determine the area being metered, and they are useful for measuring specific parts of the scene from the camera position. If you are shooting a singer who is lit by a spotlight on a dark stage, a normal reflective meter will yield incorrect readings if it is used from the camera's position in the

Figure 2.1: *Digital spot meter.*

auditorium. From the camera's position, the spot meter can be aimed to measure only the brightly lit singer to yield a valid reading for exposure purposes.

I have run into this problem several times at concerts. Modern professional cameras have built-in spot meters (as do higher-end 35mm and digital still cameras). Rather than taking a reflected reading at the wide angle setting, zoom into a close-up and take the reading. Some cameras require you to press a button labeled "spot meter" to achieve this. This is the only accurate way to obtain the correct exposure.

This is one of the few, extreme instances where I will not use a light meter and rely only on the camera's internal metering system. It might prove difficult jumping up on the stage and holding a meter in front of the talent. I trust the camera for the most part, but nothing beats taking a reading at the source.

But why use a light meter at all if this form of metering is the same as the camera's auto iris system and the WFM, which gives you very precise and accurate measurements on any section of the scene? The reason is that it is far more portable than a camera and WFM, and will permit you to light a scene without having to set up expensive video gear and pay a technical crew to stand by while you do your thing. Final decisions about exposure can be made once the camera system is up and running. At that time, you can use the camera and WFM to give you absolute assurance of the end results and to make critical decisions about the final look of a scene before rolling tape.

Incident Light Meters

Incident light meters are used by standing near the subject and aiming the meter's light-sensitive cell toward the camera (see Figure 2.2). The cell may be covered with a hemisphere or a flat disk of some translucent material. The purpose of this translucent material is to filter out certain wavelengths in the spectrum that could cause the cell to give incorrect readings. Just as the television camera must be aimed at a standard white card during white balance (see Chapter 1) to produce an accurate color signal, light meters are calibrated against a standard at the time of their manufacture.

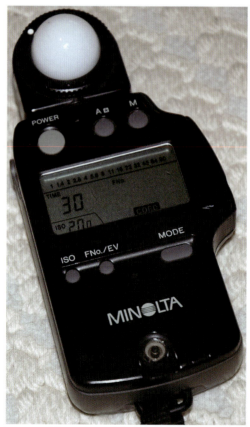

Figure 2.2: *Digital incident meter model auto meter VF.*

They are calibrated to express accurate exposure readings when the light being measured is reflected from the surface of an 18% gray card. The dome or disk, known as a diffuser, converts the incoming light to the 18% gray card standard. If the diffuser were not in place, the light would shine directly on the cell and result in a nonstandard reading.

The hemisphere, or dome diffuser, allows you to measure light from as great an angle as 300° so you can measure all the lights focused on a subject.

The flat disk diffuser has a narrower angle of acceptance, usually about 50°. This allows you to measure the output of a specific instrument that is aimed at a subject lit by multiple instruments.

As you take your readings, be sure to aim the disk or dome toward the camera. Especially in the case of the domed meter, do not block any of the light that would normally fall on the subject in the position you are metering. The domed meter is particularly helpful when you are trying to set and focus individual instruments used to light an actor's blocking. (Blocking is the path that actors are asked by the director to take when moving from point to point on the set.) It is important that you know where actors will be moving during the shot before you begin your lighting setup. Face the cell of the meter toward the camera and walk through the blocking to see the combined effect of all the instruments. (Many meters allow you to swivel the cell portion of the meter so you can see the reading from the back side of the cell while it is facing away from you toward the light).

You can let the meter guide you in your instructions to the grip (see Chapter 13 for an explanation of a grip's role) in terms of the placement and focus of each unit. Lighting intensity can be consistently maintained throughout the blocking pattern if that is your intent, or you may wish to create areas of light and shadow. Walking this path lets you determine hot spots or dark areas on the set.

Placing the dome on the meter is helpful when you are taking readings to determine the exposure ratio of the set so that you can establish and maintain lighting continuity from shot to shot. If you walk to the foreground of the shot and take a reading, you can adjust the light to your predetermined level. Then you can move to the background area of the set and adjust the light so that you can maintain your predetermined ratio for that scene. We will discuss ratios and continuity in the next section of this text.

Videographers, unlike filmmakers, have other tools available to help them determine what the exact results of their efforts will be. I still use the same Sekonic Light Meter (see Figure 2.3) I purchased in college. Although it is old, it is still used by many professionals because it is a trusted analog meter that is both reflective and incident. This versatile instrument is used on every one of my shoots—film or video. Unlike most digital meters that display an exact f-stop, an analog meter makes you do the math to determine the correct stop—but it never needs a battery, like a digital meter.

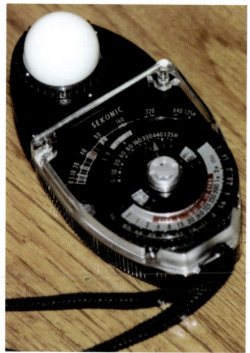

Figure 2.3: *Analog incident/reflective meter.*

Now we will discuss a second instrument common to video as well as still and motion photography.

Color Temperature Meters

Just as the intensity of light can be measured with a light meter, the color spectrum of light can also be quantified through use of a color temperature meter. One of the easiest meters to use for this purpose is the Minolta Color Meter III F. Its relatively high cost may be a valid reason for not having one of your own in your gadget bag, but there clearly are times when one should be rented for site surveys and actual shoots where you will be confronted with light sources operating at a variety of color temperatures. As indicated in Chapter 1, it is important to know the relative amounts of red, blue, and green light in the various sources that illuminate your scene.

The color temperature meter is used in much the same way as an incident light meter. The meter's diffusion disk is aimed toward the source in question, and a built-in microcomputer memorizes several important factors about the light source. When you push the button marked "K," the actual color temperature is digitally displayed in degrees Kelvin in the meter's readout window.

When you push the button marked "CC," the meter displays the color compensation index in a plus or minus figure. A reading of +3, for example, would indicate the need to filter a cool white fluorescent source with a $\frac{1}{4}$ Minusgreen filter to balance with a 5600°K daylight setting on your video camera. The correct filter to use for a given reading is indicated on a chart that is printed on the back of the meter. Although the chart is calibrated for film rather than video, a free Cinegel overlay that correlates the values displayed by the meter with Rosco's video filtration media can be obtained from Rosco. This overlay is the same size as the chart on the back of the meter and can be peeled from its backing and stuck over Minolta's chart.

Often, when a specific mood is desired, your color temperature could swing in a different direction than the norm. In a period film I shot about the early 1930s, I wanted all of the interior scenes to be warm and inviting—or in other words, an orange cast. By balancing to tungsten with a color temperature meter and then dimming the lights to 70%, I achieved the orange glow I was after. Although I could not determine this with my eye, by using the color temperature meter I saw that my light level would be orange. The result can be seen in Figure 2.4.

If you push a button marked "LB" on this meter, you will get a reading indicating the correct light-balancing index for the source light. For example, a reading of—131 would correlate to the need for use of Tough Blue 50 to boost a 3200°K lamp to match existing daylight sources accord-

Figure 2.4: *Warm glow in a 1930's period film.*

ing to the Rosco overlay mentioned earlier. The letters "CC" or "LB" will appear in the window along with the index number so there is no confusion regarding which area of the conversion chart you should refer to.

Knowing exactly which conversion filter materials to use in order to color correct for various mixed color temperature sources can save a great deal of time and money when you are faced with difficult lighting situations. Earlier color temperature meters were more difficult to use and designed in such a way that an error in reading the analog displays or interpreting charts was likely to contribute to some problems in selecting the correct filter material. The digital meter, combined with recent developments in filter material, makes it possible for good color correction to be made on location in seemingly impossible situations.

Besides the fact that it's costly, some won't use a color temperature meter because they believe the video camera will sort it all out. Most cameras will do an excellent job of this, but film cameras must still rely on the meter or the exposed film must be color corrected (either at the lab or in post production). It may be worth your while to rent a color temperature meter and take readings on your set. Sometimes these subtleties will improve your video with correction filters.

Additional Tools

Videographers have three tools unavailable to filmmakers which assist in achieving proper exposure and color balance: (1) the color picture monitor, (2) WFM, and (3) vectorscope. Used properly, these tools can guarantee results. They may also be responsible for the failure of some people in video to really learn their craft.

There is a tendency among some video people to think the camera's auto white circuits will take care of problems involving sources with mixed color temperatures, that the auto iris will take care of exposure, and the zoom lens will permit convenient camera location to get the shot quickly. What more could you want? All cameras now focus automatically.

Accomplished film people would laugh at such thinking. They will have specific goals in mind when a scene is shot and be concerned about such things as depth of field, contrast ratios, exposure ratios, film stock, filter packs, lens focal length, camera angle, etc.—things that some video people do not consider or even know about. Film people have been in the business of exposing life to a recording medium for a great deal longer than video people have, and they have learned their craft well.

There should be no arguments between practitioners of the two media. They share common problems and can use common solutions. Each medium has its own unique advantages. Perhaps if the motion picture industry had grown up with all the automatic tools commonly available to today's video crews, they too would have become as lazy as some members of the video community.

Besides having access to the light meter and color temperature meter used by film crews, video lighting directors have the color picture monitor, the WFM, and the vectorscope to guide them in determining proper exposure and achieving a specific look.

The purpose of discussing these technical aspects is not to make you a technician. It is intended to give you an understanding of how these tools can assist you to consistently obtain the look you want. It will also prevent you from being bullied by the technician whose solution to all problems is to demand more light. You should know what the system can and cannot do. Generally speaking, if your color monitor is properly calibrated, what you see is what you will get. There may be problems in the nonvideo areas of the signal (such as sync and blanking) that require technical attention, and the WFM and vectorscope will assist the technician in discovering and correcting them.

Color Monitor Setup Procedures

The WFM will provide you with the greatest amount of technical information about your setup, but a properly adjusted color monitor is your best friend when you are making decisions about the aesthetic aspects of the picture. Most of the new consumer analog and digital cameras offer a color viewfinder or pull-out color monitor. These monitors are not the same and should not replace a calibrated color monitor because it is nearly impossible to adjust these LCD color viewfinders correctly (most do not even have adjustments). Only the lower-end digital, consumer-grade analog and digital-video formatted (DV) cameras have color viewfinders. The higher "pro" models still use black-and-white because it is easier to focus.

With a properly adjusted color monitor you can ask: Is the depth of field what you want? Are the exposure ratios correct? Does the lighting lead the viewer's eye to the center of interest? Is the mood of the scene correct? Can you see the detail you are looking for? Is the picture noisy in the dark areas or overexposed in the highlights? These last two aspects can also be determined by using the WFM.

You need an accurate, calibrated visual indication of the camera's signal. You should invest in a high-quality monitor because cheap color sets will not render colors accurately and are, in fact, designed to mask noise and other factors that are sure to show up on good monitors in the post-production suite later on.

When working at a TV station shooting commercials, we always carried a 3-inch, portable color monitor to make sure our Betacam SP footage looked alright. The camera didn't have color playback, so we relied on checking the color signal from the camera's video output. Everything always looked great on that monitor because the image was so small, the resolution so sharp, and most problems were masked. When we got back to the editing suite, the footage never quite looked so great.

Once the monitor has been properly set up using the correct test signals, it should be left alone. If the scene does not look right to you after monitor setup is complete, change the lighting, the f-stop, or some other aspect of the camera setup until you achieve the look you want. Diddling with the monitor will do nothing to correct the problem, and it will make any later evaluations you make with that monitor invalid.

I have been on location when the client looked at the monitor and said that they did not like the look of the shot. They wanted more detail in the dark areas. Instead of changing the lighting or some aspect of the camera setup, they adjusted the monitor until they saw what they wanted! The controls on the monitor should not be used to "improve" the picture.

Using Test Signals

As mentioned in Chapter 1, the camera produces a proper color signal based on its ability to reproduce white. White is the reference used in the auto white balance procedure. A similar situation holds true with a color monitor. The technician should begin the setup by making sure the set is properly converged so the red, blue, and green guns are not misaligned. Once that is accomplished, continue the setup procedure using a monochrome or black-and-white signal. A gray scale generated by a signal generator is preferred, but if you do not have a test signal generator, you can play back a videotape of a black-and-white movie or a gray scale produced by a signal generator. If you use a black-and-white movie, you should select a scene that contains black areas, gray areas, and white areas. If the monitor introduces any color or tint into the picture from your monochrome signal, adjust the screen and gain controls of the monitor.

You may be tempted to shoot the chip chart with your color camera to perform this test, but this would not provide a true black-and-white signal, and if the resulting image on the monitor showed signs of color anywhere, you could not be certain if the problem was the result of improper monitor adjustment or incorrect camera encoder setup.

Unfortunately, there is no scientific method of establishing precise monitor setup in the field. Even though there is still room for error in the first method described here, using test signals will provide far better results than will any random adjustments based on subjective viewing of regular program material. The second method, employing SMPTE (Society of Motion Picture and Television Engineers) color bars, is extremely easy and accurate. This method is described below.

Color Bars

This next step in the setup process is subject to error caused by your visual perception, but it should be reasonably accurate. Using the monochrome signal, adjust the monitor's brightness control for proper levels of the black areas of the picture. The details in those areas should be readily apparent. If the monitor is equipped with cross-pulse capabilities, activate the cross-pulse signal and adjust the brightness so that the blackest picture area is just slightly brighter than the blanking area (see Figure 2.5). This is one adjustment that will change from location to location, depending on the ambient light falling on the face of the screen. Naturally, you should

Figure 2.5: *Image from a cross pulse monitor and blanking information.*

try to position the monitor so that neither bright studio lights nor the sun will wash out the picture.

Before continuing, a word about color bars. There are three basic types of color bars generated by cameras and test equipment. The first standardized bars conformed to the Electronic Industries Association (EIA) standards of 1967. Technically, they are RS-189 bars, commonly known as "full-field bars," illustrated in Figure 2.6. These were revised in 1976 to become RS-189-A bars, commonly known as "split-field bars" (see Figure 2.7). Though both versions are intended for use in setting up color monitors, among other things, they are not very well suited to the task. They serve other test functions far more efficiently than providing a standard for color monitor setup. During the monitor setup procedure just described, it was assumed that a version of EIA bars was all that you had available.

In 1978, an SMPTE committee report recognized the shortcomings of EIA color bars with respect to monitor setup and proposed the color bars shown in Figure 2.8. At last there was some science to an otherwise educated-guess procedure for monitor setup. As with many good ideas, this one about an improved form of color bar was not widely accepted until recently. I cannot imagine why.

In the field, color bars will be generated by the video camera. All professional and most semi-professional cameras have this feature. Sony's DV and DVCAM cameras, as well as ½-inch and above CCDs generate EIA full-field color bars.

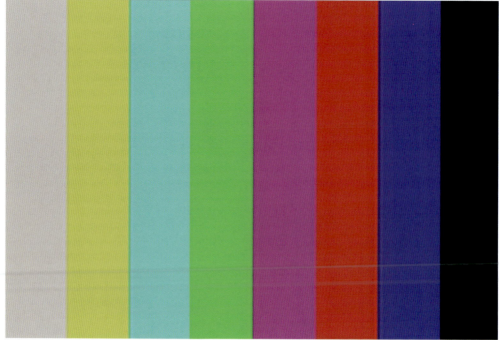

Figure 2.6: *EIA full-field color field bars (RS-189).*

Figure 2.7: *EIA split-field color bars (RS-189-A).*

Figure 2.8: *SMPTE color bars.*

A simple and accurate brightness setting can be accomplished using the SMPTE color bars. Brightness is set with the aid of the three vertical black mini-bars that are located in the lower right-hand corner below the main red bar of the signal. The three black bars are very close in value specifically to provide a reliable key to brightness adjustment.

The left bar of the trio is just a bit blacker than black. The small center bar represents true black. The right bar is just slightly brighter than true black. The idea is to adjust the brightness control of the monitor so that the bar on the left cannot be seen. If it is visible, the brightness control setting is too high. If the bar on the right cannot be seen, the brightness control setting is too dark and should be brought up just enough so the right bar is visible. At the proper setting the blacker-than-black mini-bar and the center, true black bar will not be visible. Only the whiter-than-black bar should be visible. This simple, foolproof method of adjusting brightness is more accurate than the cross-pulse method previously mentioned and requires less time, fewer test signals and assures far greater accuracy.

Adjust the contrast control for proper levels in the white picture areas. Details should be visible in the white areas, and the brightest white produced by the monitor should not be so bright that it causes eye strain. Like the adjustment of the brightness control, the contrast adjustment will change from location to location depending on ambient light conditions.

Color Reproduction

Once you have adjusted the brightness and contrast controls, you are ready to start making adjustments that affect color reproduction. If you use the older EIA bars, change your signal source from a monochrome tape or signal generator to the color bars from your camera or a signal generator. Obviously, the camera is the least complicated source for this signal, especially on single-camera shoots.

The two controls involved in color adjustment are the color and hue, sometimes called tint.

The color control adjusts the saturation or amount of color present. It should be adjusted so that the color bars appear normal and are not oversaturated. When colors are oversaturated, they begin to "bloom" or "bleed" into the colors that surround them.

Usually when you are looking at full or split-field color bars, the red bar is the first to bloom into the magenta bar on its left and the blue bar on the right when the color control is set too high.

The hue or tint control is perhaps the most subjective adjustment of all. The idea is to adjust the hue so that the colors appear natural—not too red and not too green. I prefer to make the adjustment watching the red and magenta color bars. When the magenta is correct, not too red and not too blue, I am satisfied with the setup. Some like to make this judgment watching the cyan bar. Your preference about which bar to use as a reference for hue setup should be based on your own sensitivity to color.

Using EIA bars, it is a bit tricky to adjust the color (saturation) and tint (hue) properly. If your monitor has a "blue only" setup switch, you should activate the setup switch so that only the blue gun displays the color bar signal. Rotate the color control so that the outer two blue bars are of the same brightness. The hue control should be adjusted so the inner two bars of blue are of equal brightness. When all four bars are of equal brightness, the monitor is properly set (see Figure 2.9).

One of the most difficult judgments to make is determining when the outer two bars are equally bright when adjusting the color control. Their distance from one another is the biggest factor in making your judgment. Since the inner bars are closer together, the hue adjustment is a bit easier. No matter how good a job you think you have done using EIA bars, you will find that no two people seem to come up with the same settings using the same bars on the same monitor. A better mousetrap was needed.

Here is the SMPTE solution. That narrow row of seemingly useless colors below the regular color bar display of the SMPTE signal is an ingenious blend of tints that can be used in conjunction with a blue gun only setup switch to provide completely accurate color and tint adjustment. It is foolproof.

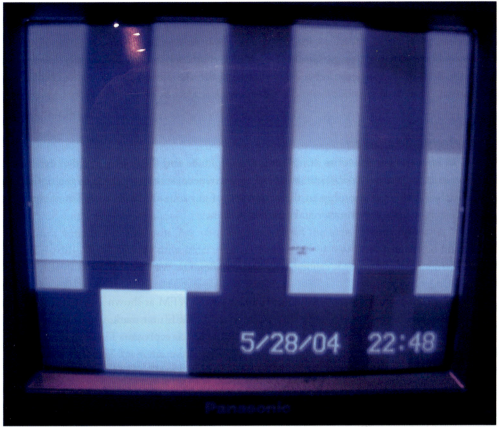

Figure 2.9: *Properly set color bars using a monitor's blue gun.*

The idea is to display the SMPTE bars using the blue gun only and adjust the color and tint controls so that the upper portion of each bar is the same brightness as the smaller section at its base. This is a very easy judgment to make since the two sections are always contiguous and the slightest discrepancy in brightness is easily discerned. When each of the seven segmented bars looks the same from top to bottom, you have accurate adjustment of the color and tint controls.

Once the monitor is adjusted, keep your fingers off the monitor controls. If the set is lit and you do not feel there is enough detail in the black areas, add more light. Do not mess with the brightness control of your monitor. If white areas of the picture are losing detail, reduce the light falling on them or, in the case of windows with natural sunlight coming through, increase the neutral density (ND) filtration. If you have no additional ND filter material available, use the color monitor and WFM as guides to stop down until you get the detail you are seeking. Then you will have to add more base light to the scene to keep the black areas from compressing to the point where excessive detail is lost in the dark areas.

Chapter 3
Lamps, Reflectors, and Lighting Instruments
What Is the Difference?

There are two basic types of illumination: specular and diffuse.

Specular illumination is the type found outdoors on a bright sunny day, when the light rays are strong, sharp, and nearly parallel to each other. As a result, they cast sharp, well-defined shadows on your exterior location site. There are also artificial sources of specular illumination for use in the studio or on exterior sets. They are carbon arc sources or specially designed discharge lamps with smooth, well-polished reflectors and some form of lens system.

Diffuse illumination is the type seen on a cloudy, overcast day when the sun's rays are diffused by the clouds to produce soft, scattered rays. Under these conditions the rays are not parallel to each other and produce flat lighting with poorly defined shadows. This type of lighting can be simulated in the studio as well, using special instruments or placing a diffusing material between the lamp of any instrument and the subject. It is also possible to create diffuse light outdoors on a sunny day, in a limited area, by placing a large piece of diffusion material, called a "butterfly", between the sun and the subject. Naturally, there is a limit to the area you can tent in this manner (see Figure 3.1).

Lamp Types

As lighting director, you have total control over the look of the finished product when you shoot in the studio, and you have a wide range of control on exterior locations. One of the first options you have is your choice of lamp types. The term "lamp" does not refer to a kind of lighting fixture,

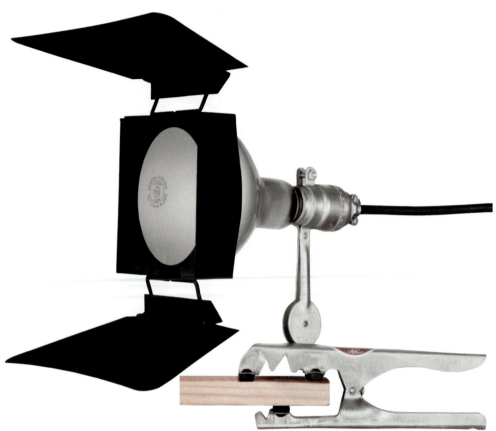

Figure 3.3: *Photoflood lamp with barn doors (Photo courtesy of Mole-Richardson Co.).*

and changed color temperature as they aged. To counteract these shortcomings and increase the useful life of larger lamps of this type, the manufacturer put sand inside the envelope. The instruments were designed to be used with the lamp burning base down. During operation the sand rested in the base. When the vaporized filament deposited a visible black film on the inside of the envelope you could shake the sand around inside to remove the tungsten film from the inner surface of the envelope. When the shaking was completed, the blackened material would settle with the sand to the base of the lamp. This first form of dry cleaning could have been called "one-watt martinizing."

Quartz Halogen Lamps

The problems of light loss and declining color temperature were solved with the invention of the quartz-halogen lamp. Currently the most common light source for interior location lighting, these lamps offer several distinct advantages over earlier tungsten lamps. They are much smaller than earlier designs of comparable wattage, making possible smaller and lighter fixtures for location lighting. The tungsten filament of these lamps is enclosed in a quartz envelope that is filled with halogen gas. The quartz envelope can withstand greater temperatures than the glass envelope, making the smaller lamp size possible.

Thanks to a man named Emmet Wiley of General Electric, who developed the halogen cycle, these lamps maintain a constant light output and color temperature throughout their lives. Even though their filament evaporates like those in common household lamps or earlier tungsten studio lamps, it is constantly being regenerated. As a result of the halogen cycle, the evaporated tungsten is never deposited on the inside of the envelope. Instead, it is redeposited on the filament to maintain consistent output and color temperature.

The majority of quartz-halogen lamps have clear envelopes and produce specular light with their relatively small filaments that are enclosed in short quartz envelopes (see Figure 3.4).

If you want softer, more diffuse light on the set, there are quartz lamps designed to produce less specular light. These lamps have a longer tubular shape to provide greater filament area (see Figure 3.5). Some have frosted and textured envelopes to diffuse the light further. Though some of these lamps are used in broads that produce a fairly harsh light, others are used in fixtures designed to provide softer, more even illumination such as scoops or softlights.

Even though these lamps produce a softer light, I still do not consider them to be a diffuse source unless they are housed in a softlight. Any other open-faced instrument, such as those commonly found in location lighting kits, will require the use of diffusion material in front of the lamp to produce a truly diffuse light.

A couple of points to remember when working with quartz lamps: Never handle them with your bare fingers. The oil from your skin will react with the quartz envelope and cause a blister to form on the quartz envelope when the lamp is turned on. The blister will expand until the envelope explodes. Obviously, this could harm people and material on the set. Always use gloves to replace lamps, or use the paper or foam cover that comes with each lamp. If you do touch a lamp by accident, or if you aren't sure if someone else may have touched it, you should clean the lamp with a soft cloth soaked with isopropyl alcohol. Even if you take these precautions, point open-faced fixtures away from people and set decorations when you first turn them on. This will minimize the harm done, should it explode.

When installing the longer, tube-type lamps that have contacts on both ends, you may wonder where to place the small bump that exists on the surface of the lamp. This is a result of the vacuum-sealing process in manufacture and it does not make any difference whether this seal is facing the reflector or the front of the instrument.

You should pay close attention, however, to the manufacturer's instructions regarding the correct operating position of the lamp base, up or down. Failure to follow these recommendations will substantially shorten the lamp life and may cause damage to the instrument's socket.

Figure 3.4: *Quartz-halogen lamps.*

PARs and FAYs

Two types of quartz-halogen lamps, PARs and FAYs, are constructed like the old sealed-beam automobile headlamps. That is, the filament and reflector are sealed together in a quartz envelope, with the front surface of that envelope acting as a lens and the silver-coated neck of the lamp acting as an internal reflector. They are manufactured to provide one of three basic patterns of light distribution: spot, medium flood, or wide-angle flood. If you need to change the focus of

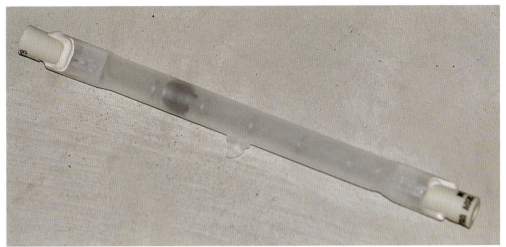

Figure 3.5: *Tubular quartz lamp.*

instruments using these lamps as light sources you must install new lamps of the appropriate focal length. The PAR lamp is a 3200°K source (see Figure 3.6) and the FAY lamp is a 5600°K source because of a dichroic coating on the front surface of the lens. This coating has a tendency to wear off and cause a shift in color temperature as the lamp ages or as the result of being touched during installation, setup, strike, or packing.

MR-16s

One of the newer applications of modern technology to television lighting is the development of MR-16 lamps (see Figure 3.7). The first versions of this lamp were intended for use in 35 mm slide projectors, but the focal point requirements of such an application made them inappropriate for use as a general-purpose light source. Originally designed by Emmet Wiley, MR-16 lamps consist of a quartz-halogen capsule permanently mounted in a multimirrored ceramic reflector bowl. The reflector has special optical coatings that permit the majority of infrared and ultraviolet radiation to pass through it.

The redesigned version suitable for general lighting purposes is the result of additional design work by George Panagiotou of Cool-Lux and comes in 12-, 14.4-, 30- and 120-volt sizes ranging, from 50 to 250 watts. They are available in a variety of prefocused ranges: narrow spot, spot, narrow flood, and flood (see Chapter 11).

As with all quartz sources, you should not touch the lamp capsule of these units with your fingers. When handling these lamps, it is also important not to touch the inside surface of the special mirrored reflector. The integral reflectors are chemically coated to provide very efficient projection of the visible light spectrum forward while allowing the infrared and ultraviolet radiation to pass backward through the reflector and be vented out the top and rear of the instrument, away from the talent.

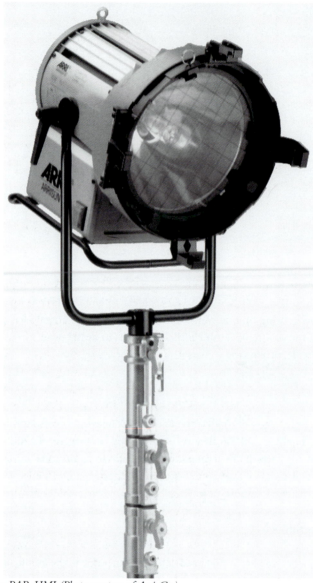

Figure 3.6: *Arrisun PAR HMI (Photo courtesy of Arri Co.).*

Carbon Arc Lamps and Carbon Arc Fixtures

The carbon arc lamp is the closest thing we have to true point source light and consists of a gas-filled quartz envelope containing two carbon electrodes. A high-voltage DC current is discharged between the electrodes to produce an intensely bright light that is color balanced to daylight temperatures. These lamps are used in expensive, bulky instruments that are not suitable to most small-budget interior location work.

Figure 3.7: *MR-16 lamps in LE mini-strip (Photo courtesy of Light & Electronics, Inc.).*

Carbon arc fixtures are historically larger and much older than units using carbon arc lamp sources. Although rarely used today, they were used outdoors because they do not have envelopes around the carbon electrodes, and are referred to as plain carbon arcs. Since the arc is not enclosed, it is necessary to vent the resulting fumes away from the operator and the talent. Because of the need to have a technician to service each instrument during operation and the need for a high-voltage DC power distribution system, it is unlikely that you will be involved with such light sources for the average television production. If you tape a theatrical production in an older auditorium you may run into carbon arc sources in their follow spots. These spots have their own DC power converter built in to the base of the unit and are generally vented through flexible tubing to the outside or some ventilating system. Since the other light sources in the production will probably be balanced for 3200°K, a color correction filter such as a Tough MT/Y will be required to convert the follow spot to tungsten color temperature. The exact color correction material required will depend on the type of carbon rods being used. Consult the carbon rod package for details and filter the output accordingly.

My only exposure to a carbon arc lamp has been in a projector at a drive-in theatre. The two carbon arcs in the projector had to be brought together until they ignited, then backed off slightly. Throughout the movie, this "light" had to be constantly adjusted as the carbon arc burned to produce a bright and proficient image on the screen. The vapors, the constant alignment, and the thorough cleaning afterwards made me glad that they have been replaced by more efficient units.

Discharge Lamps (HMI)

Used with increasing frequency for location lighting (and all the time in Hollywood) and a safer replacement for the carbon arc, the HMI discharge lamp offers several advantages over other types of light sources. It is a man-made discharge lamp that comes close to being a true point source. There are other forms of discharge lamps, like mercury vapor or iodine street lamps, that produce extremely poor spectrums for photographic purposes. The HMI discharge lamp, however, is designed primarily as a photographic source with a spectrum well-tailored for the job. Many of the earlier objections to these light sources, like flicker or erratic output, have been overcome and they now deserve your serious attention as a possible light source for interior or exterior location work.

This highly efficient lamp produces 5600°K light with a unique day-lite spectrum and a high CRI. (The CRI is a number assigned to light sources, indicating their ability to render test colors accurately. The higher the number, the more desirable the source.) The HMI discharge lamp contains an optimum combination of various metal halides of rare earths. The quartz envelope contains rod-shaped tungsten electrodes to produce an arc from the extremely high DC voltage supplied by an external ballast. Like other quartz sources, these lamps should be handled with the same precautions. While the HMI system is more costly to purchase or rent than conventional instruments, and each instrument requires its own rather bulky ballast to boost the standard 110 VAC to the required high-voltage DC, it offers other economies that must be examined before eliminating it from your lighting plan (see Figure 3.8).

Unlike other quartz sources, HMI discharge lamps cannot be used immediately after they are turned on. They require a short warm-up period before they reach the correct color temperature.

Also, as a result of the ballast involved, they cannot be dimmed electrically the way quartz-halogen sources can be.

Consider these statistics from a manufacturer's data sheet. A 575-watt HMI instrument has the light output of a conventional 2000-watt unit with a daylight filter. A 1200-watt HMI equals a 5000-watt conventional unit with daylight filter, and a 2500-watt HMI equals a conventional 10,000-watt unit with daylight filter.

Economy is relative. How else could you put 10,000 watts of light on a set using two instruments and two 15-amp circuits without melting the talent and having to gel a window in the shot with 85 gel? The answer is that you could not. And it takes less time to set up and strike two instruments than it does to deal with five or more instruments and the multiple shadows they produce.

The more expensive HMIs could mean that you do not have to rent a generator, plus they produce less heat than their less expensive counterparts. HMI lamps also have a longer life than quartz-halogen lamps. All things considered, HMIs can be far less costly in the long run. Hollywood has been using HMIs exclusively for years; whether the production is shot on film or tape, the HMI is a highly desirable light source. HMI lights will be discussed in greater detail in Chapter 4.

Reflection

In addition to lamp selection, another important factor that determines light quality is your choice of reflectors. Understanding some of the physics involved will help you select the best reflector and instrument type to achieve your desired results.

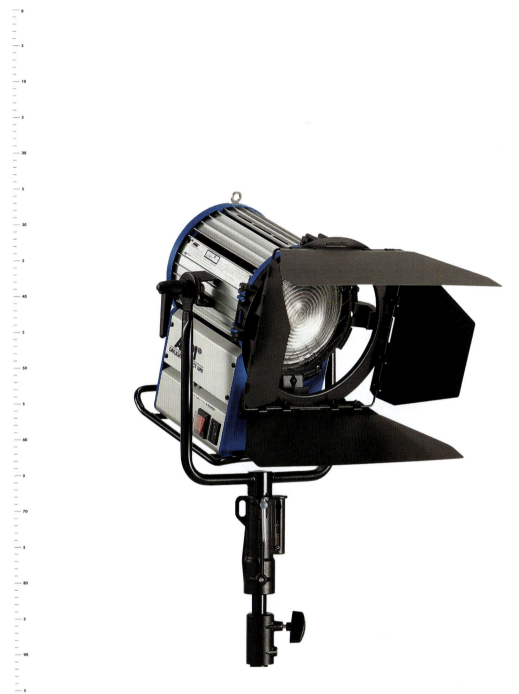

Figure 3.8: *Arri Compact 1200-Watt HMI (Photo courtesy of Arri Co.).*

Figure 3.11: *A Blanket-Lite on the set.*

External Diffuse Reflectors

When the reflector is textured and breaks up the light that strikes it, we have diffuse reflection (see Figure 3.12). Unlike specular reflectors, diffuse reflectors always change the quality of the light that falls on their textured surfaces. The reflected light produces less harsh shadows and lessens the color intensity of the subject. We will examine that effect shortly.

Since the final quality of an instrument's output is determined by the combination of lamp type, internal reflector type, and lens type, if any, when you want a very harsh light for a scene you should begin with a specular source (a small area filament in a clear quartz envelope or HMI lamp) and a specular reflector. A carbon arc spot would be an even more specular source.

Less specular light is produced by a combination of a specular lamp and a diffuse reflector. The softest light possible is produced by using a diffuse lamp and large diffuse reflector arranged in such a way that the lamp is never visible from the front of the instrument.

Internal Instrument Reflectors

Reflectors serve several functions in lighting instrumentation. They gather, concentrate and direct the light from the lamp. They determine the efficiency of the instrument in terms of its ability to

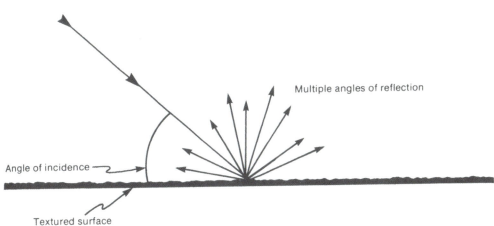

Multiple angles of reflection

Angle of incidence

Textured surface

Figure 3.12: *Diffuse reflection.*

produce the greatest candlepower per watt. They affect the "throw" of the instrument, or the distance it is able to project light efficiently. They also determine the quality of the light. There are several characteristics of reflectors that can be generalized.

The size of the reflector affects the quality of the light. Smaller reflectors tend to produce more specular light. Larger reflectors tend to produce more diffuse light.

The shape of the reflector affects the focal point of the instrument, its coverage area, and efficiency. There are five basic shapes for reflectors, shown in Figure 3.13, in order of their light-gathering efficiency. For purposes of illustration they are all assumed to be specular reflectors.

The texture of the reflector affects the quality of light as well as the instrument's throw. A smooth, polished reflector produces a specular beam. It is used in instruments that must be placed great distances from the subject.

A shiny, randomly textured reflector produces a somewhat less specular light with medium throw and is ideal for use in key lights.

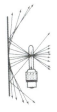 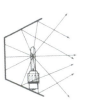  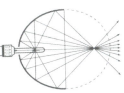

Flat   Angled   Parabolic   Spherical   Ellipsoidal

Figure 3.13: *Reflector shapes.*

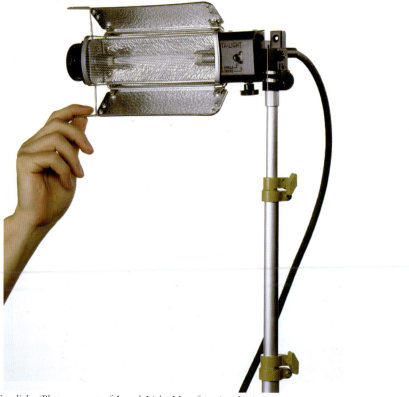

Figure 3.19: *Tota-light (Photo courtesy of Lowel-Light Manufacturing, Inc.).*

flat, even fill light. Careful placement of nooks can add a great deal of depth to sets by providing separation of scenic elements (see Figure 3.21).

Broads serve well as a source of sunlight through set windows and doors. They can be grouped together and placed behind a diffusion material such as tuff spun or rice paper to provide simulated sunlight like that found on a cloudy day. If you do not diffuse the broads they will create a more specular source that casts more well-defined shadows on the set like sun on a cloudless day.

Scoops

Unlike broads, scoops are not very portable (see Figure 3.22). They are large, round instruments with diffuse, parabolic reflectors. Some have gel frame holders that permit the attachment of barn doors and color or diffusion media. Some have a focus control. They produce a very soft light. Their large size and soft, uncontrollable output make them impractical for most location work. If ceiling height and transportation space permit, they are an excellent choice for base light and fill applications in high-key scenes because of the ease in blending their coverage areas. This same

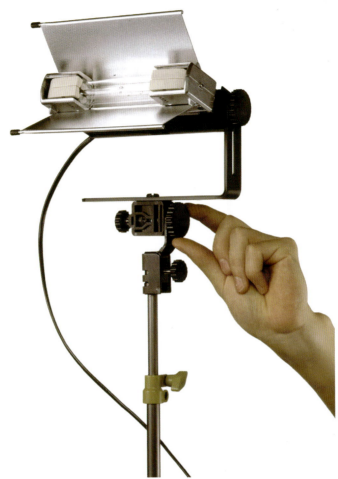

Figure 3.20: *V-light (Photo courtesy of Lowel-Light Manufacturing, Inc.).*

characteristic would make them a poor choice for low-key scenes where precise control of spill is a must. Scoop lights were a favorite in television studios.

A smaller form of scoop that can be very useful on large location sites, as well as some of the smaller ones, is the utility light. Though it is sold in hardware and department stores under a variety of different names, it is nothing more than a small, aluminum reflector bowl (from 9 to 12 inches) with a standard household lamp socket. Generally they have some wimpy metal clamp attached with a ball and socket arrangement so they can be clamped on the edge of something and aimed at the subject. You can use the various-wattage photo lamps and photo floods in these little wonders to supplement lighting in a variety of locations. They are also an effective means of placing a little light overhead in small areas of a factory or warehouse. Remove the clamp and suspend them on a lamp cord over the area of action. They can be painted and hung within the shot. If you carry a few with you, you'll find a variety of uses.

Figure 3.23: *Softlight (Photo courtesy of Mole-Richardson Co.).*

Figure 3.24: *Portable softlights (Photo courtesy of Lowel-Light Manufacturing, Inc.).*

specular than that provided by a traditional softlight source, but it is still a very good means of softening light on the set.

Softlights on a much larger scale are available commercially. They may be called "cones" or "overhead clusters" and are commonly used for lighting automobiles and other shiny-surfaced subjects (see Figure 3.26). Generally they contain one or more lamps that are shielded from direct view and their output is directed toward the inner surface of a large matte white box-like fixture. They are often used with diffusion material covering the opening to further diffuse the output. The distant sibling of this cluster is found in fast food restaurants to keep food warm.

You can create effective cluster lights on the set by using Foam core to construct a large, open, box-like container. Once you have taped the five pieces together, place the unit several feet from

Chapter 4
What's Out There in Lighting

There are a lot of different lighting units available from the major dealers. So how do you know what is what and how it can possibly help on your production? This chapter, although not an exhaustive list, will discuss a wide variety of lighting units and what specifically sets them apart from the rest.

To fully know what each manufacturer has to offer, go to their corresponding website (listed in each section) and get a catalog. I will list each company alphabetically and describe a few of their more popular units.

Arri

A maker of high quality 16 mm and 35 mm cameras, Arri (www.arri.com) offers a wide selection of Fresnels, fluorescents, and HMIs. Beginning with their HMIs, the smaller units, 125 watts offer more punch than a tungsten light four times its size. Advancing to the 200-, 575-, 1200-, 2500-, 4000-, and 6000-watt models, you will have an arsenal that is unmatched.

The tiny three pound 125 watt Fresnel HMI produces an outstanding 1872 foot-candles of daylight at a distance of 5 feet. For something that takes up so little space, output of this magnitude was unheard of a short time ago. This light definitely warrants mention because of its size and power (see Figure 4.1).

The next unit is one of my favorites on a shoot because it is powerful enough but still mobile with its ballast. The Arri 1200-watt Compact HMI blasts 8000 foot-candles of light at a distance

Figure 4.6: *Chimera Video Pro Plus Lightbanks (Photo courtesy of Chimera Co.).*

out-perform 650-watt Fresnels and open-face 1000-watt lights using 150-, 250-, or 300-watt configurations. When the daylight balance filter is attached to the unit, its output competes with a 200-watt HMI.

Cool-Lux's SL 3000 is a softlight that is mounted on the camera. Using a 100 watt lamp mounted so it bounces off of the back of the unit, it comes in either AC or DV configurations.

A unique light, only from Cool-Lux, is the U3. With a three-lamp configuration (two floods and one spot), these quartz 3200°K lights have a life span of 2000 hours.

Kino-Flo

A name known for fluorescent lighting, Kino-Flo (www.kinoflo.com) specializes in flicker-free daylight and tungsten-balanced fluorescents. One of the most amazing things about Kino-Flo lights is their versatility.

On a commercial shoot for a regional client, we had to illuminate a salad bar and make it look appealing as well as appetizing. Although we had a food stylist, our tungsten lights would illuminate only certain facets of the food—leaving other areas too dark. The answer to this problem was

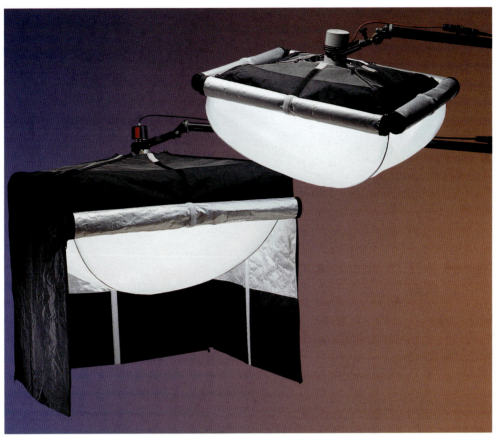

Figure 4.7: *Chimera Pancake Lanterns (Photo courtesy of Chimera Co.).*

using Kino-Flo Diva Lights. Available in several bank configurations (two-, four-, eight-lamp, etc.), we could place these wide, even lights on the backside of the salad bar and shoot through the front. Salad bars are normally lit with fluorescent lights above the food, but these are rarely color balanced to the correct temperature and leave the food looking too green or red. With tungsten-balanced Diva Lights, we now had a correctly balanced salad bar.

The client wanted a slow dolly shot revealing all of the sumptuous food littering the tufts of green. Tom Landis suggested we replace the fluorescent salad bar lights with the tubes from our Diva Lights. This is versatility! Each fluorescent tube of the Diva Light was removed and attached to the same size holder in the salad bar (see Figure 4.8). When illuminated, we now had color-corrected practicals that still functioned as a unit. Before the Diva Light came along, this would have been a much more difficult shot.

The smallest 12-volt Micro-Flo, these lights are cool enough to hold in your hand but bright enough to illuminate someone in a car.

Figure 4.8: *Replacing the salad bar lights with Diva Light tubes.*

With lamps in both 3200°K and 5500°K, these 4- to 6-inch lights are thinner than a pencil and flicker free. An object placed 2 inches from the source still receives 130 to 146 foot-candles. A Pepper would cook any object that close to its lamp.

While shooting a short video, all of the action took place in a traveling car. To light this epic, we drove the car onto a trailer and towed it everywhere with the actors seated inside. All of our lighting was Kino-Flo fluorescent. The actors in the front seats were both lit using one daylight-balanced Micro-Flo gaffer taped to the dashboard, and the rear seat passengers each had their own units hung from the headrests.

Although these Micro-Flo units were AC powered, an AC/DC converter (something about the size of a car battery), changed the AC to a more convenient battery-powered DC. Each Micro-Flo was dimmable (without changing the color temperature) and was attached to a ballast, which in turn went to the AC/DC converter (see Figure 4.9).

The Micro-Flos, because of their size, acted more as fill lighting while two Kino-Flo Four Bank Select lights were mounted to the hood to act as key lighting (see Figure 4.10). These units could

Figure 4.9: *Micro-Flo lighting in use on a car's interior.*

Figure 4.10: *Kino-Flo fluorescent lights mounted on a car's hood.*

Figure 4.15: *6000-Watt Molequartz Spacelite (Photo courtesy of Mole-Richardson Co.).*

Kit Lighting

I believe almost every manufacturer makes a "lighting kit." This usually means they have decided to put their best-selling lights into a convenient package than can be carried from place to place. I don't have space to mention what every company offers in its complete line, but here are a few examples.

Arri Kits

As with most manufacturers, their most popular lighting instruments are available in kit form. Even HMIs, like the Arrisun and Pocket PAR, come in kit form, with various wattage lamps and units. Numerous Fresnel kits—or, my personal favorite from Arri, the Softbank 2—may be purchased. This is the kit I use. It contains 1K with diffusion, two 650-watt Fresnels, and one 350-watt Fresnel. With stands, barn doors, and screens, you have a portable, 90-pound lighting arsenal.

Figure 4.16: *2000-Watt Molequartz Molette (Photo courtesy of Mole-Richardson Co.).*

Cool-Lux Kits

Soft Kits I, II, and III come strangely enough with the same number of large softlights in each of the corresponding kits. These kits feature a Combo-Light with 300-, 500-, 750-, or 1000-watt lamps. The largest kit, the Soft Kit III, includes three Combo Lights, two Mini-Cools, and one Micro-Lux On Camera Light. As with any manufacturer, these kit specifics might change over time, so it is best to contact them directly for the most recent configurations.

Lowel Kits

Lowel has been making kits forever, and most of us started in this business (back in the early '80s) with a Lowel Kit. Today, they offer VIP, DP, Omni, Tota, Fren-L, Rifa-Lite, and Multi-System kits. They are available in almost any size and configuration, so contact the manufacturer for kit specifications.

Figure 4.17: *Softlight kit (Photo courtesy of Arri Co.).*

Other Lighting Instruments

A variety of lighting instruments exist that can be used on location or in the studio. Location equipment can easily be used in the studio because it is portable and a snap to set up. The only drawback is that they may lack the power or "punch" that studio lighting provides. Studio lighting may be used on location, but some of the instruments may be too cumbersome to drag to the shoot.

Mole-Richardson, Lowel, Arri, Cool-Lux, Kino-Flo, and several others have developed "kits" that contain several lighting instruments, stands, and grip equipment in a convenient (but heavy) carrying case (see Figure 4.17).

Mole-Richardson also makes smaller versions of their studio lights for location work, such as the 600-watt Teenie-Weenie Mole, 650-watt Teenie Mole, 1000-watt Mickey Mole, and 2000-watt Mighty Mole. Most quartz instruments over 2000 watts are difficult to manage and power on location.

Fluorescent Lighting Units

The more lights on a set, the higher the temperature. The only way to illuminate objects without raising the heat level is to use fluorescent lighting fixtures. These units are not the same instru-

Figure 4.18: *Florescent fixtures in a salad bar.*

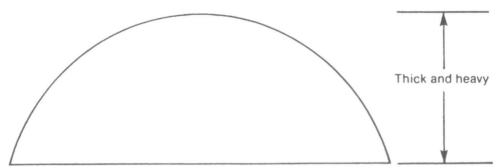

Figure 4.20: *Plano convex lens.*

Knowing a lens must have nonparallel surfaces to redirect light, the first lens makers produced a plano convex lens (see Figure 4.20). Such lenses are thick, heavy and break easily. Since the aspect of design that makes them function is the fact that the back surface is not parallel to the curved front surface, it is reasoned that you could remove the center section of the lens as long as the portion extracted had parallel surfaces (see Figure 4.21). This results in a stepped lens, which can bend light in the same way as the heavier plano convex unit can because the back surfaces of the lens are at the same relative angle to the front as they were in the plano convex lens. So much for the excess weight. But we still have a lens that requires the same depth from the farthest rear surface to the front of the curve.

Fresnel reasoned that if the key factor in redirecting light is the difference between the angles of the two surfaces, then it should be possible to slice up a stepped lens and place all the rear surfaces of each step in a straight line, leaving the front surfaces with their original curvature. In this way you have the Fresnel lens—a flat, thin lens that has the same light-bending characteristics as heavier, thicker, fragile plano convex units (Figure 4.22).

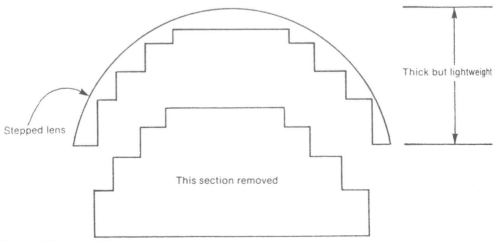

Figure 4.21: *Stepped lens.*

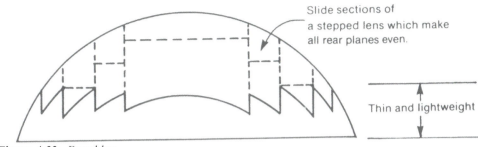

Figure 4.22: *Fresnel lens.*

In a Fresnel instrument, the lamp is backed by a spherical reflector located at a fixed distance from the filament. It redirects the light to a focal point at the plane of the filament, producing a single focal point for the reflector and the lamp. Remember, the location of the focal point for a reflector in an open-faced instrument changes in relation to the filament focal point as it is moved to affect focus. This creates two focal points and produces multiple shadows.

To change the focus of a Fresnel from spot to flood, the lamp and reflector together are moved closer to the lens (see Figure 4.23).

All Fresnels provide for the addition of color media holders, scrims, barn doors, and snoots to give the designer maximum control of the output. Instruments start as small as 3-inch, 100-watt Inkys and range up to 25-inch, 20,000-watt units. The 3-inch designation refers to the diameter of the lens. Like the open-faced focusing spot mentioned earlier, Fresnels have a good range from spot to flood (see Figure 4.24).

Lekos

The Lekolite, commonly referred to as an "ellipsoidal" because of its reflector shape, was invented by Messrs. Levy and Kook, who founded Century Lighting and gave the instrument its name. Lekos offer the most precise focus of light output. When absolute control of spill is mandatory, the Leko is often the best choice. The reflector is a specular ellipse so the light output is specular, but it can be modified with filter material to achieve a diffuse quality. A wide variety of lens

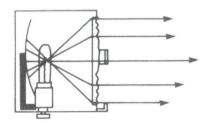
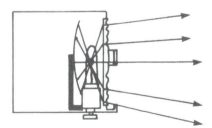

Figure 4.23: *The spot and flood focus of a Fresnel.*

Figure 4.27: *2000-Watt Molelipso (Photo courtesy of Mole-Richardson Co.).*

Regardless of which form of Leko you rent or own, a common problem is reduced light output due to poor alignment of the filament in the elliptical reflector. Rented instruments are especially plagued by this problem. It is not uncommon for Lekos to be so misaligned that their output is reduced by 66%. If you have worked with certain instruments at a given throw and wattage on a number of occasions, you will know what their output should be. If you have no previous experience with an ellipsoidal instrument and end up renting one that is misaligned, you will probably not detect the misalignment unless there is gross error in the filament placement. As a result, you may install a higher-wattage lamp (which may only add to the alignment problem), or you may add additional instruments to bring the intensity up to the desired level.

Lekos are very precise optical instruments, and even a slight deviation from the intended position of the filament in relation to the reflector results in great degradation of light output. A misaligned filament not only reduces output but affects the quality of the coverage pattern. Instead of producing an even field of light, a misaligned instrument will produce hot spots, dead spots, and color aberrations and may even project an image of the filament on the talent or set walls or floor.

Alignment problems result from harsh handling, or the replacement of lamps or sockets. Even when a lamp is replaced with one of similar wattage, there is enough difference in the orientation of the new filament to reduce output. When the new lamp is of a different wattage entirely, the chance for misalignment is even greater. You can align the lamp properly using the series of screws on the outside of the lamp holder at the base of the lamp. The idea is to place the filament along the optical center of the reflector at the focal point, which is situated at a very precise distance from the back of the reflector.

The alignment screws in most older instruments cannot be adjusted easily and do not appear to be any more than fasteners that hold the lamp housing together. The latest designs from Strand and Colortran, however, provide a joystick at the base of the lamp to make alignment simple. More-efficient heat sinks on the socket keep the instrument cooler during operation and extend lamp and socket life. To make an alignment gauge, cut a rectangle of 16- to 22-gauge sheet metal to the exact size of the color frame holder of the Leko to be aligned. Use a #50 drill to make a small hole in the exact center of the metal rectangle. You now have your alignment gauge.

Place the instrument about 3 feet from a white wall, with its beam perpendicular to the surface of the wall. Insert the alignment gauge in the color frame holder and darken the room so you can see the image of the filament and the reflector projected on the wall through the small hole of the gauge. With a poorly aligned instrument there will be light and dark areas of the reflector caused by the incorrect filament location. By adjusting the four or five screws in the cap of the lamp housing, you will be able to realign the filament within the reflector. The object is to move the filament to the center of the reflector. When it is properly aligned you will see the bright glowing areas of the reflector increase in number and in area. When you have maximized the bright areas of the reflector and created an even pattern of light on the wall, remove the hot gauge with a pair of pliers and aim the instrument at a wall 25 feet away. You should see a much brighter, even field of light. If not, some minor adjustments of the alignment screws may be necessary. Generally it will not require further work.

This procedure gives you the brightest flat field of light possible. If you need more light for your particular situation, you can increase the light output in the center of the pattern by moving the lamp slightly forward in the reflector. This involves an equal adjustment of the three or four perimeter screws and a tightening of the center screw in the lamp base. To gain light in the center of the projected pattern you will have to sacrifice output at the edges and a darker ring will appear there.

These instruments are commonly designated as 6 × 9 s or 8 × 8 s, etc. The first number in the designation is the diameter of the lens in inches and the second number indicates the focal length of the lens.

Lekos, in combination with other materials, can create an interesting background pattern. An example of this combination would be to place a Leko on the ground and run some white mesh fabric from the base of the light to the top of your set (see Figure 4.28A). With a colored gel in the light, point the unit so it illuminates the fabric. You now can see the trail of that color light as it travels along the mesh as shone in Figure 4.29. Figure 4.30 shows a slightly different angle

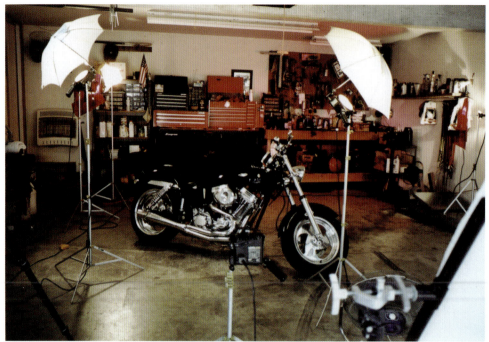

Figure 4.32: *Lowel kit light and a motorcycle.*

It is rare today that most location shoots cannot be lit with the contents of a kit or one of the newer forms of lighting mentioned in this chapter. Chapter 12 will discuss several specific lighting situations and how I lit them. I will then ask, as an exercise, for you to come up with two different ways of lighting the same situation: one using the units I did, and the other using different ones. Use this chapter as a reference as to what each lighting instrument can do for you and apply that knowledge in Chapter 12.

Chapter 5

Video Contrast Ratios

Help, They Don't Match!

"Contrast ratio" refers to the maximum allowable difference between the brightest area of the picture and the darkest. While film can accommodate ratios as high as 100 to 1 (i.e., the brightest object may be 100 times brighter than the darkest object), television is commonly considered to have a contrast ratio of 20 to 1. Current technology has improved this ratio to 30 to 1, and 50 to 1 in HDTV. The use of CCDs and improved circuits are the reasons for this increased range. From a practical standpoint, you should still work with the 20 to 1 ratio, however. This gives you a 5 f-stop range. If you try to use a contrast ratio higher than the standard you are working with, your images will degrade. It is best to work with a lower contrast ratio than the medium's standard you are currently working in.

Limited contrast ratio is frequently used as an excuse for not being able to produce aesthetically pleasing pictures. That is hogwash. You can create a great sense of depth and produce very good-looking pictures working within the limits of the transmission system. The earlier problems of extreme highlights causing pictures to bloom and distort have been almost completely eliminated because of CCDs. CCD cameras can handle highlights 6 to 8 f-stops above 100 IEEE units and can shoot in the "night mode" (0 Lux). Unless you are shooting live outdoor events, over which you have no lighting control, there is no reason to tax the system with contrast ratios it is incapable of handling.

Table 5.1: *Contrast to f-Stop Conversion*

f-Stop Range	Contrast Range
1	2:1
2	4:1
3	8:1
4	16:1
5	32:1
6	64:1
7	128:1

pepper and colored splotchy noise. The "night shot" cameras I mentioned earlier in the book were designed to let the consumer record their child's birthday party in candlelight. However, even if we were creating that exact same scene in the studio, we would still use conventional lighting.

If the brightest element in the scene is 100 IEEE units or peak white level, the rest of the picture will obviously ride up and down as manual or automatic adjustments are made. Because we are working with a 30 to 1 contrast range, 30 steps down from that peak amplitude is the noise threshold of the system. The noise does not go up or down by adjustment of controls; it just sits there. And to make matters worse, every time your nondigital master tape is dubbed down a generation, the threshold level of this noise is raised by a contrast step or two.

You can use the camera as an expensive light meter to determine the contrast range in a scene. Zoom in to a tight close-up of the brightest area of the scene and determine the f-stop for 100% amplitude on the waveform monitor or until the zebra stripe appears in your viewfinder. Now repeat the measurement looking at the darkest area of the scene. The f-stop range you identify translates into a contrast ratio by a base 2 power law (see Table 5.1).

Now you can see how improper lighting translates into noisy pictures. If your scene has a 5 f-stop range and a highlight suddenly appears and drives the auto iris down 2 f-stops, your remaining contrast range is now no better than 8 to 1. Any scene elements below that threshold will be driven into the mud. All you see on the screen is system noise.

On the other side of the coin, if your scene has only a 2 or 3 f-stop range from peak white to black, the picture is going to look flat and washed out, with very little color saturation, if the auto iris opens up in search of some highlight.

Lighting Ratios

Lighting ratios are determined by comparing the intensity of the key light to that of the fill. (If you are uncertain about key and fill lights, turn to Chapter 6.) Generally, only a small area of the scene, such as an actor's face or body, is involved in computing a lighting ratio. Once that ratio has been established for a given position on the set, it should remain the same throughout a series of shots in that area. While the actual position of the key and fill light may change in height or horizontal angle to accommodate movement from shot to shot, the ratio between the two should not change so that the shots will match when spliced together. You may wish to change the intensity of the key and fill to control the depth of field in a series of shots. These changes will present no problem when the shots are cut together in post so long as there is a proportional increase or decrease in both the key and fill to maintain the same ratio between the two.

High Key

The lighting ratio between key and fill is important in establishing the mood of a shot. If the key light measures 160 foot-candles and the fill light provides 80 foot-candles at the subject's location, you have a high-key setup with a 2 to 1 lighting ratio. Take special note that there is an inverse relationship between the term "high" key and the "low" ratio used to achieve it. In high-key shots the ratio of key to fill on the subject is low, like 2 to 1 or 3 to 1. High-key ratios are usually used in comedy and nondramatic situations. Backgrounds in high-key shots are generally brighter than those in low-key setups. The overall effect of high-key lighting is brighter shots with less texture. The look is similar to what you would expect when shooting outdoors on an overcast day.

Though it has been stated that backgrounds are usually brighter, by definition, in high-key shots, they do not figure into the calculation of a lighting ratio. They only come into play when exposure ratios are calculated (see "Exposure Ratios" later in this chapter.) There is nothing to prevent high-key lighting from being employed in front of a black backdrop.

Low Key

Low-key ratios are used in more dramatic situations in which the inverse ratio of the key to fill is high. An example of dramatic low-key lighting would be a situation in which the key light measures 200 foot-candles and the fill measures 25 foot-candles. In this case, the ratio would be 8 to 1. The result is deeper shadows and a more textured look. Lighting ratios deal only with modeling light on the subject, but as a general rule, low-key shots are involved in scenes in which the background is at a lower intensity than the background used for high-key ratios on the subject. More specular light sources are used for both the subject and the background when low-key ratios are being used.

If a lighting ratio has been determined by the lighting director, simply take a meter reading from the key light—let's say it's 400 foot-candles. If the lighting director wants a 4 to 1 ratio, the fill light must be 100 foot-candles. Aim the light meter at the fill light and move the light until the reading is 100 foot-candles.

When shooting video film-style, it is important to maintain the same lighting ratio throughout a series of connected shots in order to preserve continuity and make the shots cut together smoothly during post. Generally we think of continuity as something that deals with props and costumes being in the same positions from shot to shot (and this form of continuity is very important), but continuity of lighting ratios is of equal, perhaps greater, importance. With multicamera, real-time television production, such as sporting events or award shows, continuity is automatically maintained. When video is shot film-style, lighting each shot separately as filmmakers do, failure to keep track of lighting ratios can become a big problem in post, especially if a series of connecting shots is made over a period of 2 or more days.

The lighting ratio alone is not the only factor that determines the mood of the shot. In Chapter 7, we will examine a number of stock setups that can be used to convey mood and time of day. Changing the position and direction of the key can have just as great an influence over mood as the ratio involved can have.

Determining Lighting Ratios

There is a variety of ways to determine an appropriate lighting ratio for any scene. The biggest influence should be the subject matter of the script and the way it is being dealt with. The director's intent and the elements of the set should also influence your approach. You may be asked by the director for a 2 to 1 high-key setup, or you may be told to work at a given f-stop in a high-key or low-key situation. Whatever the criteria, you will need to know the proper techniques for metering your setup.

Depending on the size of your crew and the setup involved, you have a couple of choices regarding metering techniques. You can use your incident light meter, with the flat diffuser disk or the hemisphere dome. If you are using a setup in which the fill light is positioned in front of the actor, instead of being off to the opposite side of the key light, the fill will also contribute light to the key side of the subject. In such cases, you should turn off all the set lights except the key and fill and take a meter reading using your incident meter with the hemisphere dome in place. Place the meter in front of the actor's face and point it toward the camera. Take your reading. Say it is 250 foot-candles. That is the key, or "K" value, that will be used in the formula that follows. Next, have an assistant turn the key light off, and take a reading. This time it is 85 foot-candles. That is the value of your fill, or "F" value. Now let's determine the lighting ratio (LR). Using the formula LR = K/F, LR = 250/85, or LR = 3 to 1 (approximately).

This technique is time and labor intensive because of the need to first switch all set lights off except the key and fill and then eventually switch off the key light. This is because the hemisphere dome will accept light from a wide angle, as much as 180°, and you do not want other set lights to contaminate your reading. That same factor also makes it possible for you to get an accurate reading of the combined key and fill lights to get a true value for the intensity of light that will be striking the actor on the key side. Once that value is known, you must measure only the fill light to calculate the correct ratio.

A metering technique that is much quicker and less labor intensive involves the incident light meter and the flat diffuser disk. In this case, the reduced angle of acceptance eliminates the need to kill all the set lights except the key and fill. To determine the lighting ratio, point the flat disk directly at the key light and move the disk around slowly. You will notice a slightly higher reading in one specific position. Use that high reading as the K value in the formula. Next, aim the flat disk directly and the fill light from the position of the actor's face. To avoid turning off the key, you can use your hand to shadow the key light from the disk. As before, move the meter slightly to determine the highest reading from the fill light, making sure you continue to prevent the key light from falling on the disk. Make note of your F value and compute as before.

Exposure Ratios

The exposure ratio (ER) is the figure that indicates the brightness differential between two or more areas of the same scene. It is not the intensity difference between two instruments, the key and the fill. If you want, you can think of it as a lighting ratio on a grander scale. A typical example would involve measuring the intensity of light on the acting area and making another measurement of the intensity of the background. If the background is lit fairly evenly, only one measurement is required for the entire background. If the background is lit unevenly as the result of windows or practical lamps on set, these areas should be measured separately.

For example, if an effect light is projected on the back wall of the set to simulate sunlight streaming through a window on screen right, that area of the background will be brighter than the screen left area of the back wall that does not have a projected effect. We would expect screen left to be darker because of the absence of effect projection and the natural falloff characteristic of light. To illustrate, we will call the screen left section of the background area 1 (A1), the screen right area of the background area 2 (A2), and the acting area center screen area 3 (A3) (see Figure 5.1).

Because exposure ratios involve the intensity of larger areas lit by more than one or two instruments, meter readings are always taken using the spherical diffuser. You want to measure the effect of all the instruments that contribute to the intensity of a given area. When you meter an area to establish and calculate exposure ratios, use the spherical diffuser with all set lights for the master or wide shot on at operational levels.

You want to be able to determine the ratio between various areas that will be involved in the scheduled shots. The formula is ER = Al/A2. The intensity of each of these areas involved should be measured while aiming the meter at the camera with all the set lights operational.

If the shooting schedule calls for a master wide shot, two medium shots, and a close-up, as shown in Figure 5.1, you will need to meter the three areas involved. You do not have to maintain the same foot-candle readings in the two areas involved in each of the narrower angle shots, but the ratios must remain the same. You may want to decrease the light in area 3 and area 2 to reduce the depth of field for the close-up of actor B. The intensities can be lowered, but the ratios between the areas involved must remain the same to maintain lighting continuity.

When shooting indoors, where you have complete control over lighting ratios and exposure ratios, you should have no trouble staying within the 30 to 1 contrast ratio of the television system.

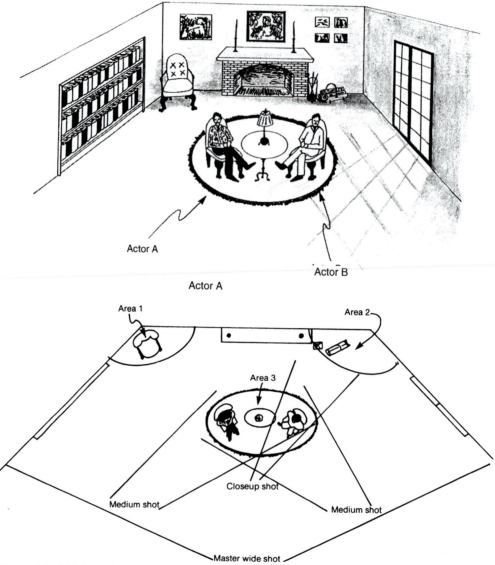

Actor A

Actor B

Actor A

Area 1

Area 2

Area 3

Closeup shot

Medium shot

Medium shot

Master wide shot

Figure 5.1: *Lighting ratios.*

Problems may be caused by the nature of the subject, such as extremely shiny objects. Those reflections can be reduced by treating their surface to control the potential problems.

Problem highlights from highly reflective subjects can be controlled by reducing the light that strikes them with dots, fingers, flags, scrims, or nets, or by spraying them with dulling spray, hair spray, or certain types of a light dusting of spray paint of the appropriate color. Matte silver gaffer tape can also be used effectively on some silver subjects to reduce glare. Naturally, any paint you spray on a subject must be tempered by the disposable nature of the subject. Shiny bald spots and high foreheads on talent can be treated with Arrid Extra Dry deodorant spray or baby powder to reduce glare and stop perspiration; the unscented variety is preferable. For purposes of tact, glue a plain paper wrapper around the can before taking it on set, and tell the talent you are using a special material to improve his on-camera appearance, if he asks any questions. Outdoors, the use of butterflys, scrims, and fill light can bring contrast ratios under control. We will examine these accessories in detail in Chapter 7.

Chapter 6
Instrument Functions
What Do They Do?

Before we can discuss instrument placement, it is necessary to define eight primary instrument functions. Depending on where instruments are placed, their relative brightness, and the areas they light, they perform different functions. In one instance, a Leko may be positioned far upstage and aimed at the back of a rock star, serving as a backlight. In another application, that same instrument may be located downstage, projecting a cloud on the cyc and functioning as an effects light. The functional uses suggested here are only general guidelines. In reality, your backlight may function as a key with just a bit of front fill. The specific setup will be dictated by needs, conditions, and location limitations, plus the aesthetic requirements of the script.

Key Light

The title of this book is *Placing Shadows*. One reason for that title is to emphasize the importance and necessity of shadows in good lighting; where you "place" the shadow makes a big difference. The instrument that provides the biggest clue to the location of the presumed light source is the "key light." We may delve deeply into the hidden meanings of the word "key", but let's just say that this is the most important light. Because its intensity is greater than any other light on the subject, it will and should create shadows. The angle and density of shadows serve as clues to the type and location of the presumed source. They also provide clues to time of day and the nature of the source.

If an exterior scene is extremely bright and has harsh shadows falling at a steep angle, it would not be unreasonable to assume that the action is taking place around noontime on a sunny day.

By the same token, an exterior scene that has softer shadows falling at a very oblique angle in a warm light is likely to be taking place either during the early morning or late afternoon hours.

We would expect to see well-defined shadows falling at a steep angle at noon on a cloudless day. Therefore, we place a specular lighting instrument high overhead to imitate the sun at noon, and the angle of the cast shadows determines where the instrument is placed. Later in the day we would expect the sun to be lower on the horizon, casting more oblique shadows, so we would lower the instrument to cast an appropriate shadow angle. Instrument location is determined by the mood we wish to create, the basic setup we are working with and any motivating or practical lights that are in fact, or are presumed to be, the source of light for the scene.

Do not underestimate the importance of the statement, "any motivating or practical lights that are in fact, or are presumed to be, the source of light for the scene." This is a very important consideration in setting the key light. You should not always think in a traditional manner regarding key-light placement. If the subject is walking away from the camera down a long narrow hallway toward a glass door leading to an exterior location, the key light should actually be a strong back-light. Always use the situation to determine location and type of key-light instrument.

If the location is an office without windows, we expect to see softer shadows and, therefore, would choose a softlight source or would heavily diffuse the light from more specular instruments.

The mood or atmosphere of a scene evokes a certain emotional response from the viewer and is established by the exposure and lighting ratios used by the lighting designer. Low-key scenes—and I am not referring to the height of the key light instrument—create a dark and somber mood, while high-key scenes are associated with happy, energetic situations. Using the cast shadows as your guide, the first thing you do is place the key light. The prominence of the shadows created by the key light is affected by the type of light source, specular or diffuse, and by the amount of fill light you add. Background and backlights, along with effects lights, help to complete the illusion.

Your choice of lighting setup will be based on how you wish to model or illuminate the facial features of the subject or the contour lines of the product. The most flattering setup (the portraiture setup) is one in which the key light is directed down on the actor from an angle that casts a small shadow of the nose directly below it or toward either side of the nose by the nasolabial folds, or "smile lines." It does not matter if this key light is placed on the right or left of the subject.

Since the key is generally assumed to be the apparent light source of the scene such as a window, table lamp, overhead lights or the sun, we must analyze these elements of the scene when choosing the key's location. If a preceding long shot established a bright table lamp on screen left, you would be ill-advised to key the subject from screen right in a close-up even though the lamp in question is not part of that shot. As mentioned earlier, the side the key light is placed is not important, but once placed or established, you should remain consistent.

Traditionally, a Fresnel or open-faced focusing spot will be used as the key instrument. It is a specular source that can be diffused and shaped with accessories and the focus control to provide the degree of sharpness you want from cast shadows. If you dim the key to get the intensity you want for the f-stop you desire to shoot at, you will destroy the color temperature and consequently the flesh tones. It is advisable to re-lamp the instrument with a lower-wattage lamp to establish the desired level. It is true that you can reduce intensity by using scrims or neutral density (ND) filters. They do not change the color temperature, but they do cause you to use more electricity than you need. This, in turn, adds needless heat to the location. You may also be able to take advantage of falloff and move the key farther away from the subject to reduce its intensity. Or, using LED or fluorescent lights will keep the heat down, and use less power in the process.

Using hot, mega-watt lamps is now a thing of the past when lighting people. Unless the only units available are of these heavy-power consumers, most of us have switched to using the softlight as a viable key-light source. Unlike more traditional key instruments, the softlight is not as controllable with respect to spill and shadow intensity, but it can be used as a key source. This is especially advisable when the subject is prone to severe specular highlights such as those found on highly polished metal objects, or on foil- or cellophane-wrapped products. Softlight is also more flattering to the face of subjects, especially if they have age lines or skin imperfections.

As an example of the key light used alone, see Figure 6.1. In this photo, the only light source is the key light. For the sake of this demonstration, a Mole-Richardson 2000-watt, 10-inch Junior was used. There is no diffusion on the surface of this Fresnel. Obviously, moving the light to the left or right, or up or down, would change the appearance, as would diffusion or a different lighting instrument. George Winchell created the look of this lighting test.

Fill Light

Placed in front of or on the opposite side of the subject from the key, the fill light's job is to establish the desired lighting ratio and control the density of the shadows created by the key. It should not be strong enough to create its own opposing shadows. If it does project shadows, it becomes a second key and destroys the illusion.

In the hallway example previously mentioned, the fill may be nothing more than a soft-light aimed down the hall from the camera position to provide just enough detail in the actor's clothing or on the walls of the hall. It may also be that you want no fill at all, if it is a dramatic situation. Just use the silhouette against the strong backlight that functions as the key.

Because of its quality, a softlight is usually chosen as a fill-light instrument since it is unlikely to create conflicting shadows. Its intensity can be controlled by scrims or diffusion material placed in front of it or by switches that control individual lamps in the instrument. You will still have the inherent problem of controlling spill from this instrument. If you are working in a confined area in which a softlight's spill would add too much light to the background to permit you to control the desired exposure ratio, especially in low-key situations, you can use a heavily diffused

Figure 6.1: *Key light only.*

focusing spot. So long as it is diffused sufficiently and does not match or overpower the effect of the key, it would be the better choice since its lens system makes it possible to minimize spill.

The fill light should be placed near the camera at eye level to prevent it from casting its own shadows on the subject's face. While this placement eliminates one potential problem, it might create another. It may cast a distracting shadow of the subject on the background. If this occurs, there are several things that can be done to correct the situation.

You could diffuse the light further to lessen the severity of the cast shadow. If that does not produce an acceptable result, you could move the instrument closer to the subject. Less distance between the subject and a diffuse light source will soften the cast shadows.

If you are unable to move the fill closer because of intensity problems or the fact that it might enter the shot, you can try moving the subject and the fill farther away from the background. This will also lessen the density of the shadow that falls on the wall. When all else fails, try a more directional source and position the cast shadow to an area of the close-up that will be least distracting. These cast shadows are only a problem in low-key setups. High-key backgrounds generally have enough light to mask the shadow cast by a fill.

George Winchell often uses Foam core as his "fill light." This bounce source allows illumination to fill in the dark areas without providing too much light. This is also helpful in a confined space when multiple instruments are not feasible or when your power requirements cannot be met. Foam core provides a very soft source when any instrument is pointed at it. Often the illumination from the key light is enough when used in conjunction with Foam core as fill. In Figure 6.2, Foam core was used to the left of the talent to supplement the daylight streaming in through the window. Since this was a 1930s comedy, I wanted the soft, radiant look that only Foam core and daylight provide—with flattering results.

In Figure 6.3, you see an example of the key and fill light together. The fill light has "filled in" the shadows created by the key light. The fill light used is a 1000-watt Lowel Tota-Light with no diffusion.

Backlight

The backlight is the third function discussed, and it serves a very important role in modeling subjects. Since television is a two-dimensional medium, the backlight is essential to separate the subject from its background and give the illusion of depth to the scene. When used with a key and fill, it is frequently referred to as "three-point lighting." If two backlights are used, it becomes a four-point setup. In addition to providing separation, backlights add contrast. Backlights should not only be used to separate actors from their backgrounds but also to separate various elements of the set from each other to further the illusion of depth.

Ideally, the backlight is a Fresnel or focusing spot that is placed above and directly behind the subject so that it strikes at an angle of about 45° to the floor. This will require a physical separation between the subject and the back wall of the set. If the backlight is at a greater angle to the floor, it could begin to act as a toplight and cause distracting shadows and highlights on the forehead, nose or chest of the subject. If the angle is much less than 45° it could cause lens flair.

The biggest problem with backlights on location is where to hang them. Since they should be directly behind the subject, it is not possible to mount them on a stand as with the key light and the fill. If you did, the stand would be in the middle of the shot and appear to grow out of the head of the subject. If the location has a standard suspended ceiling, the easiest method is to use a drop-ceiling scissor clamp like that described in Chapter 13.

If there is no suspended ceiling you might be able to use the Lowel Tota-mount support. It is a very useful device that can be gaffer taped to almost any surface and will support a small instrument for backlighting such as the Lowel Omni or Cool-Lux Mini-Cool. The Omni light provides focus and barn-door control and provides for the use of scrims and ND filters to control intensity. In some locations, such as in a typical warehouse, the scene is staged in a large open space that does not have a back wall near the subject and has a ceiling that is too high to permit mounting. In such cases, a horizontal boom can be attached to a floor stand with a gobo head to

Figure 6.2: *Foam core used as fill (Photo courtesy of Bill Shul).*

Figure 6.3: *Key and fill light.*

suspend the instrument in the proper location. You may also install a rigging system for general lighting purposes that is supported on stands or towers, out of camera range. Find some method to get the job done.

In Figure 6.4, we did not have access to the ceiling and our white-haired talent needed a back-light. We used an Arri 650-watt Fresnel mounted on a C-stand and arm. Mounted high above the talent and pointed down, no distracting stand was seen in the shot.

Do not get the shot without a backlight just because it is too difficult to find a way to mount the light. You will not get professional results without one.

The specular nature of the backlight and the color of the subject's hair (if any) and clothing will all have an effect on the desired intensity. These factors make it difficult to establish a standard ratio between the backlight and the key and fill lights. For this reason, you should have the subject or a stand-in run through the blocking while you rehearse any camera moves that will be part of the finished take as you adjust the light. While making the adjustments, look at the picture and waveform monitor so that you are sure of the results. If you do not use this technique, you may find the backlight level is too bright or too dim to produce the desired effect.

You are also likely to discover at the last minute that the backlight creates lens flair at some point during the shot. The solution may be to adjust the barn door of the backlight or to place a flag

Figure 6.4: *Arri 650 used as a backlight.*

above the front of the lens. If the camera is stationary during the shot, the flag may be stationary also. If the shot involves camera movement, a flexi-arm or gobo arm may be fastened to the camera dolly so that the flag will travel with the camera and prevent flair. Unlike key and fill lights, you can dim backlights with an auto-transformer or silicon-controlled rectifier dimmer to achieve the degree of separation you desire. Since they light the back of a subject (the shoulders, hair, etc.), you do not need to be concerned about color temperature or their effect on the white balance of the camera. Cool-Lux and LTM manufacture compact inline dimmers to assist with this problem (see Chapter 11).

In Figure 6.5, the backlight is the only lamp illuminated. Figure 6.5A illustrates the backlight and the hair light activated. In Figure 6.6, the backlight has been added to our setup. With three-point lighting, the subject now stands out from the background. The light of choice in this example is a 600-watt Lowel Omni.

Hair Light

I tend to think of a hair light as a limited area backlight that is used in conjunction with the backlight. As the name implies, it is used to illuminate the hair and cause a nice highlight for

Figure 6.5A: *Backlight only.*

Figure 6.5B: *Backlight and hairlight only.*

Figure 6.8: *Key, fill, backlight, and hair light.*

The term "kicker" is also used to describe specular reflections that come from various areas of the set such as the glass in a picture frame, a shiny spot on the actor's face, or eyeglasses or their rims. These types of kickers are usually undesirable and can be removed by changing the angle between the object and the light, by changing the camera position, or by spraying the area or questionable item. Polarizing filters may also solve the problems of kickers. Kickers are seen as long, thin vertical spikes on the waveform monitor and will frequently cause the auto iris to close down, leaving everything in the mud.

Sidelights or Rim Lights

Sidelights are an acceptable substitution for backlights. They are instruments that are placed to one or both sides of the actor to provide separation from the surroundings. Unlike kickers, these instruments are located just in front of the actor. They result in a rim of light around the edges of the body. Used primarily for musical numbers to give dancers a light, airy quality, they can also be substituted for a backlight when it is absolutely impossible to mount one.

Background Lights

Background lights are instruments used to light the walls of a set or the studio cyclorama. Their only function is to provide a basic light intensity on the background material in a set. Since they do not light actors, they can be dimmed as a means of controlling their intensity without affecting flesh tones. Dimming also cuts down on necessary hardware such as flags, scrims, ND filters, and stands, and reduces power consumption and heat generation on location.

Background lights have a great influence on the exposure ratio and the overall mood of the shot. In smaller setups, the background light may be provided by spill from other instruments that are lighting the subjects, or special instruments may be placed around the set specifically for that purpose. Spots or floods may be used as background lights, depending on desired results.

Background lights should be placed just as carefully as any of the other instruments in the setup. Remember that you are always trying to create the illusion that the scene is lit by some primary source such as the sun, daylight coming through a window or fluorescents overhead. There may be two or more sources of light if the scene is indoors and is lit by multiple lamps in the room, or outdoors at night surrounded by a variety of artificial sources such as streetlights, marquees, electric signs, and light from the windows of buildings. Key lights are placed so that their cast shadows are consistent with those that would be cast by the supposed source of illumination for the scene. If that source is daylight through a window that is located screen right, the actors should be keyed from the right and so should the background elements.

I am always disturbed when I see sunlight coming through a window from the right and then see picture frames and bookcases in the background casting shadows toward the right or at some angle other than the cast shadows of the key. These shadows destroy the illusion and are the result of careless and sloppy background light placement by the lighting director.

Any instrument that illuminates the background and casts shadows should be carefully located so that its shadows will be consistent with those created by the key light. Do not say, "I need more light on the background." Say, "I need some light on that bookcase from the key light angle." Or say, "Those picture frames are casting a shadow straight down from the frame". Move the background light so the shadows fall to the left of the frame and down. Pay attention to detail.

Figure 6.9 has the addition of a background light. Now our subject is no longer in limbo and the set has depth. The background light is a 1000-watt Lowel DP.

Effects Lights

Effects lights are instruments that do not serve any of the previous seven functions. They are used to create an effect, such as the projection of a tree branch onto a wall of the set. They may also be used to supplement regular background lights to bring set decorations such as plants or very dark wood furniture up to desired levels of illumination. As we have seen, plants seem to soak up

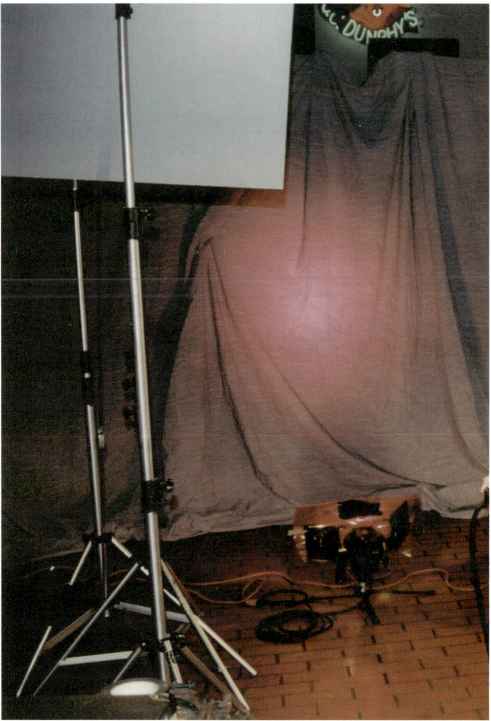

Figure 6.11: *Rose gel on background.*

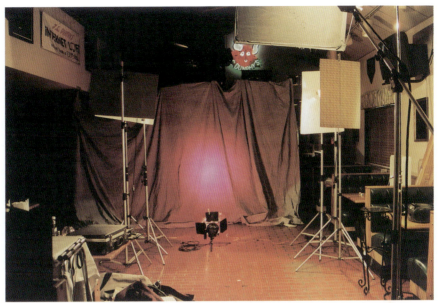

Figure 6.12: *Three point lighting with rose-gelled background light.*

Figure 6.13: *Rose gel with brunette.*

Figure 6.16: *All daylight can be a good thing.*

Figure 6.17: *Gelling Tungsten lights with amber gel.*

Figure 6.18: *The desired evening effect.*

What to Use

The question always asked is, "What type of instrument do I use for each function?" There are some common sense guidelines, but there are no hard and fast rules. Fresnels and broads make good backlights, but since these instruments may be too harsh for some scenes, you may wish to consider a zip. Fresnels and Lekos make good key lights, but again, they may be too harsh and a softlight may work instead. The fact is that lighting styles are changing, becoming more soft and cool. Today, softlights are often used for keys. Any instrument can be used for fill, providing you have sufficient diffusion material to soften the output. The selection of instrument type should be guided by the aesthetic requirements of the scene. If you do not have the ideal instrument for the job, you should have enough accessories to tailor the output of available instruments to create the quality of light you require. In the photo example of our subjects, I used the lighting instruments at my disposal and tailored them to suit my needs.

In some cases, you do not have much choice. If you want a hair light, you need an inky or small Fresnel with a snoot. Effects lights are best created using Lekos with gobos or a scene projector, but any specular source can be used in a pinch. The size of the cast shadow depends on the

Figure 7.4: *The end result.*

depth beyond that added by the backlight. The key may be specular or diffuse, but specular keys provide more dramatic lighting and a greater sense of depth. When setting the backlight, be careful not to destroy the depth you have created with this setup. Keep light off the downstage shoulder. This type of setup was used frequently in the old black-and-white Peter Gunn series to create some wonderfully eerie scenes.

With the far-side setup, placement of the key is critical because the shadows created are cast on the side of the face nearest the camera and are more obvious than in the previous situation. The key should be placed so that the nose does not cast a large shadow on the downstage cheek and the actor can move freely without casting odd shadows on the downstage side of the face. Though the basic effect will change as the subject looks toward the key and back toward camera, there will still be sufficient modeling to keep the mood. If the subject's head turns toward the fill so far that the downstage cheek is lit directly by the key, the effect will be ruined. In such a case it is best to change the actor's blocking slightly rather than make lighting adjustments.

In the far-side setup, placement of the fill is also critical. It should slightly overlap the key area and be placed at eye level near the camera. Naturally, it ultimately determines the lighting ratio and should not be strong enough to cast its own shadows.

Best suited to low-key, dramatic lighting, the far-side lighting setup still has a wide range of effects.

As stated previously, it is best to stage your long shots before lighting the close-ups. The lighting ratios of the long shots should be higher than those of the close-ups. The far-side setup intercuts well with higher-ratio long shots, maintaining the mood, but providing additional detail in the shadow areas. Since the basic look of a far-side setup places the downstage side of the face in shadow, a ratio of 4 to 1 may be used in a far-side close-up being intercut with the long shot having an 8 to 1 ratio. Figures 7.5 and 7.6 show examples of far-side lighting.

It's difficult to show exactly what these different lighting positions do in a drawing, so an example photograph of each is given. Slight movements in the positioning of each light will change the result. It's best to try each of these lighting setups and notice the subtle and distinct differences each one creates.

Motivated Lighting

To set aside a category titled "Motivated Lighting" seems to imply that it is somehow a lighting form different from earlier categories. Since all lighting should be motivated by elements in the scene, it is merely an extension of the principles that guide the cross-key or side-lighting setups that follow and the setups already mentioned. It utilizes any of the previous setups, and it is determined by the location of windows or practical electricals on the set. Even though these natural sources may not be a part of the close-up, if light sources are seen in the long shot or are implied by dialogue, they should serve as your guide to the placement of keys, fills, and backlights around the set. Additionally, these practical sources will justify your exposure ratio between subject and background.

The use of gobos and the selection of basic instrument types should also be guided by these factors. In documentary production it is best to follow these natural source clues as carefully as possible, maintaining exposure ratios in keeping with the situation. In scripted productions you can be a little freer in your interpretation, or replication, of the natural sources. When practical

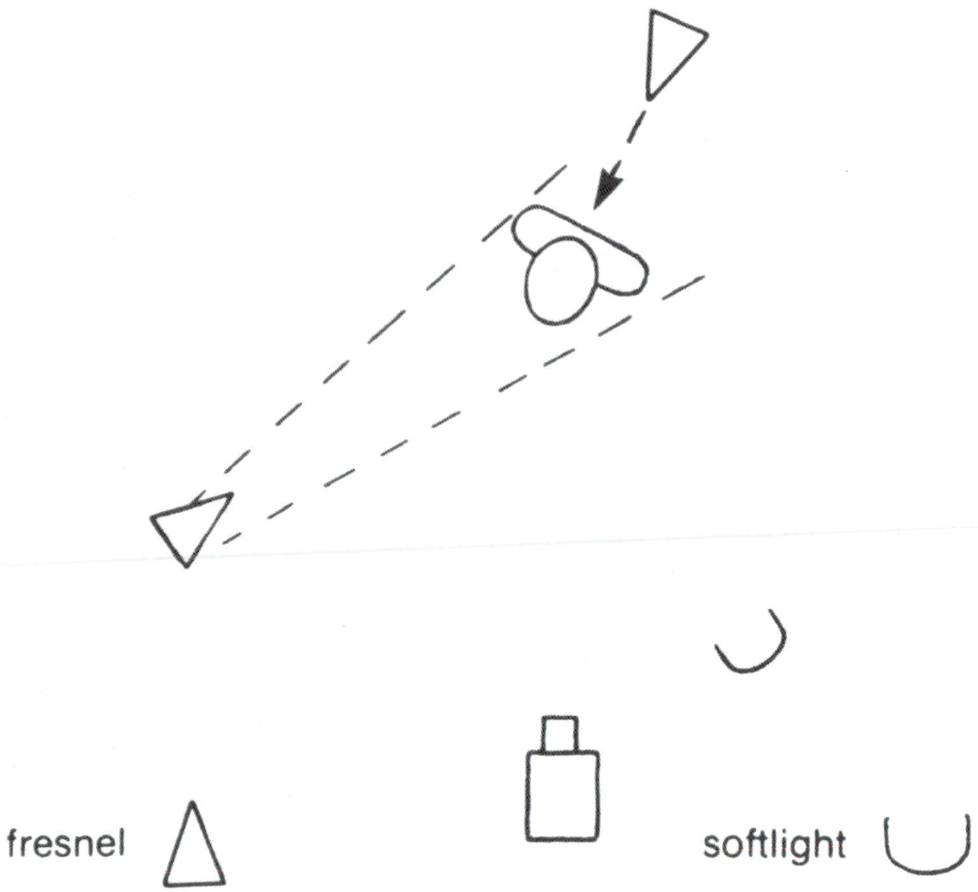

fresnel

softlight

Figure 7.5: *Far-side lighting setup.*

lights are on the set and are located in frame, use 3200°K photo lamps (see Chapter 3) and gel with neutral density (ND) filter material, if necessary, to achieve the proper exposure. Generally speaking, if a lighted lamp is visible in frame, it should be about one-half f-stop above the exposure of the subject. You should measure its intensity with the incident light meter held about one foot from the shade.

The materials, color, and texture of set walls should guide you in selecting the type and placement of background light sources. Obviously, a shiny white wall will require less light than dark wood paneling to maintain a similar exposure ratio between subject and background.

An excellent magazine (although aimed at the filmmaker) is *American Cinematographer.* Each month, the magazine shows photos of lighting techniques from feature shoots. I have honed my lighting skills over the past 20 years from reading this magazine and learning by photo example. By looking

Figure 7.6: *The desired result.*

at the photos, reading the accompanying article, then renting the movie, I have gained a new understanding of motivated lighting.

A moody, dark film like *Seven* had a unique approach to creating the gritty, foreboding look of the piece. Heavily–silked Fresnels were used to create subtle pools of light in the victims' homes. Although a dimly lit movie, the director wanted the viewer to see only what was in the pools of light, not what was lurking in the shadows.

The John Grisham film *The Pelican Brief* used an innovative approach in lighting the massive three-story lobby of the courthouse. White balloons were hung (hanging down) from the ceiling throughout the interior. Five thousand watt on 5K HMIs were then pointed at these balloons. The soft bounce lighting illuminated the southern courthouse and gave the interior a warm, hazy feel. Too many other lighting instruments would have been needed to light the behemoth interior. The balloons solved the problem.

When viewing a DVD of any Hollywood production, the "special features" section often includes how the producers accomplished something. Although rarely on lighting, sometimes a particular shot is important enough to warrant describing how it was lit. Later on, we will discuss in detail how to specifically light a few scenes with this "special features" approach.

The creation of natural, believable lighting that contributes depth and an artistic statement to the production is the challenge of any assignment. There is great satisfaction in looking at the monitor and realizing the pleasing picture you see is the result of your efforts. If you have done your job well, the amount of effort will not be noticeable, but the results will.

Side-Lighting Setups

Side lighting is used to emulate the mood and direction of various interior or exterior lighting sources. An example might involve a practical table lamp that is located next to the chair in which an actor is seated. Whether the practical lamp is seen in the close-up or not, if it is shown in a wider shot, it affects the placement of the key. The type of key light used will be dictated by the practical source itself. If the table lamp has a translucent shade on it, you could use a softlight or a diffused specular source as your key. If the table lamp exposes a bare bulb, a nondiffused key would probably be more appropriate. At any rate, the key would be located at approximately the same height as the lamp and aimed at the subject from the angle of about 90° to the talent. Naturally, you would expect the actor's face to be hot on the side facing the lamp and much darker on the opposite side. You do not need to be overly concerned about the shadows cast by such a key, as it is more important that you reinforce the effect of the real-life lighting than attempt a portraiture type of setup.

I learned an extreme example of practical lighting in film school. Hitchcock's 1960 black-and-white thriller *Psycho* has many memorable scenes. In one of the end scenes, when Norman's mother's identity is discovered, the practical lighting intensifies the effect. Mrs. Bates' form is sitting in a rocking chair, with her back to the camera. The only source of illumination is from a bare bulb directly above her head. As she is slowly turned to face the camera by a hand on her shoulder, we see that it is actually her corpse. Vera Miles screams and hits the light with her hand—sending it swinging back and forth like a pendulum. This moving shadow, the stylized music score, and Vera screaming make it a terrifying scene. The only light on the set was from this bare bulb (probably a higher wattage to ensure an image on slow black-and-white film stock). Through quick cutting we see Mrs. Bates' corpse and Vera's face in total darkness, harsh light, total darkness, harsh light—as in real life.

In the film, *Cold Creek Manor*, Sharon Stone and Dennis Quaid are being chased through their property's 1200-acre woods by "Dale," who is a bit psychotic. The only illumination appears to be coming from Dale's flashlight. As he chases our heroes, his flashlight waves wildly as he transverses the forest. Hollywood added effects like smoke so the illumination of the flashlight would be easier to see. Obviously, although 500-speed film stocks are quite common, additional lighting was needed in this scene to raise the foot-candles enough to expose the film. With clever placement of off-screen HMIs, the forest had light and it still looks as if the flashlight is "lighting the way."

As with any lighting setup designed to emulate some motivating source, you can (and should) cheat a bit to improve on the natural look, so long as you do not destroy the illusion you are trying to create. Many times, lighting directors are overly concerned about "pleasing results" and destroy the illusion they are trying to create. The temptation is to raise the key and bring it farther forward to create more pleasing shadow patterns than would be created by the practical lamp. When the cheating produces portrait-type lighting, you have gone too far. It's time to lower the key and push it back a little to get back to reality.

To lessen the stark look of such a setup, a soft fill light is placed directly in front of the subject and carefully adjusted to bring some detail out of the key's shadow area without adding any conflicting shadows. The fill can do a lot to lessen the often unflattering shadows produced by such a natural setup. The addition of the backlight will complete the illusion and separate the subject from the background. Figures 7.7 and 7.8 show a typical setup for this form of lighting.

Cross-Key Lighting Setups

The cross-key setup is merely a situation in which natural lights dictate that a second key be added to a side-lighting setup from the opposite direction. This second key should generally be of the same type as the first, and it will serve in place of the fill light. In this case there is no fill, but the backlight is still a part of the setup. Figures 7.9 and 7.10 show examples of this setup.

Cross-key setups are common in theatrical lighting. In this type of situation, two identical instruments are located to the right and left of the talent at 45° angles. One key is gelled in a warm

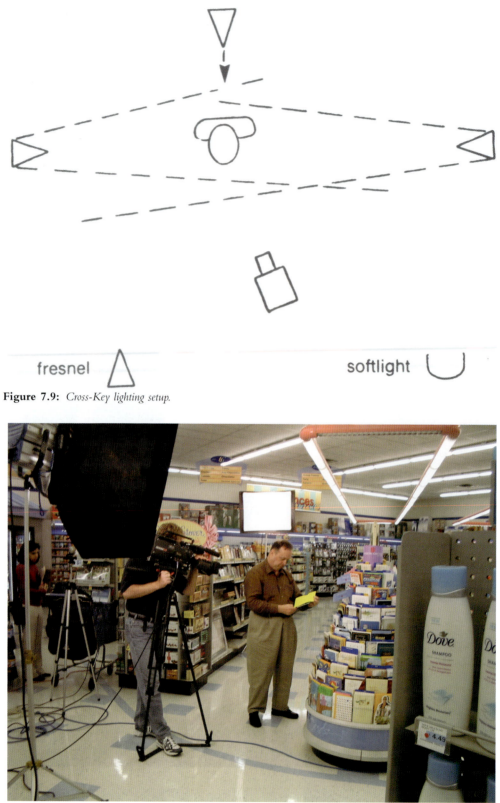

fresnel △   softlight ⊔

Figure 7.9: *Cross-Key lighting setup.*

Figure 7.10: *Cross-Key lighting at work.*

color, and another in a cool color. Because of the color difference between keys, the cool-colored key serves the function of a fill light. It creates a convincing illusion that the cool side of the talent is in shadow and establishes the warm-colored light as the key or source light.

When instruments are placed in the same relative positions to light television talent, the results are not at all convincing. Since television lights are not gelled, the theatrical effect is lost. There is no sense of where the source light is located and the end result is conflicting shadows. It's the old "Get rid of the shadow with another light" approach, and it has no place in good lighting for television.

9. A compass and watch are useful for determining room orientation and tracking the sun to learn how daylight coming through windows will affect your production.

10. Include a note pad on which to record names, titles, and phone numbers of key personnel on staff at the location. Make note of other important information about security procedures, house rules, and any unique information.

All of the above items should fit neatly in a briefcase. You can secure the necessary data efficiently and in a manner that will project professionalism to your client and/or those in charge of the location. That first impression can go a long way in greasing the skids for a cooperative effort between location owners or managers and your crew when it arrives. It is a rare owner who knows what to expect when a location crew arrives, and the more concern and respect you show for the property during the survey, the less likely the owner is to be concerned when gaffers tie into the circuit breaker panels and grips mount instruments on the doors and bookcases.

Location Complexity

In general, four levels of complexity are possible at any location. In the least complicated situations, you will have sufficient power to light the scene by simply plugging into existing outlets in the immediate vicinity. In the next case, you may find it necessary to tie in to the electrical service entrance to draw and distribute enough power for your needs. If you are still short on power, you might request that a special drop be installed by the local utility company. If that is not practical, it is time to call in an auxiliary generator. This generally requires a large, well-trained crew and a great many lighting instruments. It is at this point that you are better off calling in outside help, and since their operation will be left to those you hire, we will not discuss generator setups here.

To determine the complexity level of a proposed location, a thorough site survey is in order. Locations range anywhere from a private home to a multi-story office complex, hotel, or exhibit hall. Each has its own unique set of circumstances and restrictions that you must accommodate. Obviously, a private home with a valuable art collection and antique furniture will involve greater potential for problems than will a three-room apartment on the wrong side of the tracks. Without fail, you should have the proper insurance against property damage, general liability, and "hold harmless" clauses. Special-events coverage may be required (if obtainable) for productions shooting in locations that contain especially valuable items. In general, these rates are quite low, and you should never be without proper coverage. Check with your insurance agent before getting into high-risk situations to see if you are properly covered.

Conducting the Survey

Because of the variety of situations involved with different location sites, there is no one right way of conducting the survey, but there are some general elements that should not be overlooked.

Get the name and phone number of the person authorized to show you through the area you intend to shoot in. Make an appointment early enough so you can take any necessary corrective action on problems before your shoot date. If the site is a large multi-story building, take specific notes about its location, the nearest cross streets, and which entrance, loading dock, or elevator bank your crew is to use when it arrives. Check with building security to see if passes can be issued in advance to admit your personnel when they arrive. Get the names of security supervisors who will be on duty at the time of your shoot and meet with them personally, if possible, so they are fully aware of your intentions. Since 9/11, security is tighter everywhere, so take the extra time to get the clearances you may need.

Make a scale drawing of the shoot area on your quad-ruled pad. Indicate door and window locations and ceiling height. Indicate outlet locations. Use your compass to determine how the room is oriented so you do not try to shoot a scene at a time when the sun will be pouring into your lens or casting objectionable shadows or creating extremely bright pools of light in the area you wish to use as a background. If you plan to gel the windows with 85 gel, be sure you have accurate window measurements so you will have enough gel to do the job. Take readings with your light meter so you know what the normal light levels are in the room. If the area is lit by fluorescent lights, find out what type of lamp is used. Determine if there is a mixture of incandescent and/or mercury vapor, etc. Find out how to turn off the existing lights if they are objectionable. Sometimes they are computer controlled at some other location and no switches are available to you. Do not assume – check it out. If the lights are remotely controlled, find out who is at the switch and how to contact that person during your shoot.

There was a time when I was always carrying fuses with me to every shoot. A box full of every amperage and type (cylindrical and screw-in) was available in my briefcase. in case the inevitable happened. Now you will rarely run into a home or business that still uses fuses. The term "we've blown a fuse" has been replaced by "we've kicked the breaker." Un-kicking the breaker is as simple as removing the offending unit that caused the problem and flipping the switch back to "on." Replacing a blown fuse required a little more forethought. Fuses have not disappeared; you will read about them shortly.

Another option I used in the "old days" when shooting in a home was to tap into the 220 circuit in the kitchen or laundry. I am usually not the kind of person to "tap" into anything, but this I could handle. Most homes had (and still have) a 220 outlet for an electric range in the kitchen and one for an electric dryer. Obviously, you will not find either of these in an all-gas home. I had an electrician make up a box with four outlet boxes, each connected to a 20-amp circuit breaker. This breaker box would then plug directly into a 220 line. The plugs on a 220 line are large and unmistakable–the novice would know exactly where to plug them in. All of my lights would then be plugged into my "mini circuit breaker box," and if a problem existed, the worst thing I could do was trip one of my breakers and not blow a fuse in the house. This is a handy box to have if shooting in a home. Even if the home has a breaker box, sometimes it is more convenient to plug everything into one central location than have AC cords stretched throughout the house.

Another item that is not directly connected with lighting but should be checked during the time of your survey is the heat and/or air conditioning system. It is generally controlled remotely and may require careful planning. Again, take nothing for granted. I have been on shoots where it has taken an act of God to have the air conditioning turned off. The noise from the vents was too noisy for the audio technician. Even with pre-planning, it took quite a while before we had the system turned off. The technician in charge of the area had to be located and an agreeable solution worked out. You may need to give specific times for when you want the system turned off and back on again. Make sure you give yourself enough time; you don't want the system to start up again in the middle of your best take. If you think your shoot may wrap at 4:00, make sure the AC doesn't resume until at least 5:00.

On one specific occasion, after hearing some loud air handler units in a room we were scheduled to shoot in, I asked the house engineer if the air conditioning could be turned off during our shoot. Special arrangements were made. I met the person at the controls, got the phone extension, and felt confident that all necessary plans had been made. On the first day of shooting, I requested that the units be shut down and was told it was being taken care of. When tape was ready to roll, the noise was still there. I talked with the engineer who assured me that the air conditioning had indeed been shut down. "Then why do I still hear the air noise?" I asked. "Oh," he replied, "I have turned off the coolant, but I can't shut down the blowers. That would affect this entire side of the building." Wonderful. All the advanced planning had accomplished was to provide a noisy, hot room instead of a noisy, cool one. The moral of the story: Be specific about what you ask for from building personnel.

Ask to see the house electrician. One of your most important tasks is to determine how much power is available at existing outlets or from a nearby service entrance or power distribution centers. If you are able to obtain a current set of electrical drawings from building maintenance or electrical engineering, so much the better. It may be that you are dealing with a union house. In that case, you will have to make your specific needs known to the union steward and determine the costs involved to have their people on hand. Again, get names and numbers, and request confirmation in writing if you have any suspicion that the person in authority will not be present at the time of your shoot.

If a union does not have control, you must plan for your crew to do the job efficiently. Outlet circuits are generally 20 amps, or about 2000-watt capacity. If there are many outlets available in the area, be sure to check which breaker panels control them and how many of them are on the same circuit. If you have someone helping you with the survey, you can use a nightlight plugged into each outlet as you turn off breakers to confirm which ones control which outlet. If you are by yourself, you can plug in a small 6-volt AC/DC adapter (like those used as power supplies for radios) connected to a low-voltage buzzer. When you turn off the correct breaker, the buzzer will stop, and you can make appropriate notes. Check to see what other equipment is likely to be on that circuit so you do not disrupt power to vital equipment such as computer terminals or lab equipment.

On another shoot, I had met with the house electrician and reviewed the blueprints and electrical drawings for the auditorium where I was to shoot. The building was built in the 1920s and had the electrical service updated in the 1950s. I was told that each side of the wall could handle two coffee makers before blowing a fuse. Because tables of coffee and Danish were usually placed along the wall as refreshments for meetings, they had their electrical system based on the power consumption of these coffee makers.

Since each wall could handle only 15 amps, I needed another option to power our 2K lights. The electrician said he could provide an electrical tie-in to their fuse box (remember, this building was updated in the '50s and no circuit breaker box was available). My distribution box (four 20-amp circuits connected to individual circuit breakers) was connected directly to a 100-amp cylindrical fuse. In the middle of the lighting setup, we lost all power. Even after reviewing the electrical drawings, having the house electrician hook up my breaker box and not exceeding our amperage draw, we still lost power.

Upon examining the fuse, I noticed that it was definitely fried. After 2 hours, the electrician arrived to replace the fuse. When asked why it had blown without exceeding the draw he said, "Oh, didn't I tell you? The break room behind the auditorium is also on the same circuit. The coffee machine in the back must have turned on!" Once again, I was foiled by a coffee maker. The electrical drawings had shown that 15 amps were available in the break room, but I hadn't asked if it contained a coffee maker. The moral of this story: Ask even if it sounds like a dumb question. The mere mention of the coffee maker problem in the auditorium should have been my clue the problem could exist elsewhere. At least I learned my lesson during the lighting setup and not when the room was filled with people.

When you know which breakers control which outlets, you should then determine how much power is being drawn by other equipment on that circuit. Beware of units that draw a lot of power–like coffee makers.

The easiest way to determine circuit load is with a clamp-on AC amp meter. It has two jaws, like those of a pair of pliers, which can be opened and placed around the wire leading from a given breaker. It will indicate the current being drawn on a circuit. If the current draw is high, it may be caused by a coffee machine (what else?) or some other piece of equipment that can be turned off or relocated during your shooting schedule. Determine what the current draw is for the appliance involved and compute how much capacity is left for your lighting and technical requirements.

The way to estimate the current draw so that circuits are not overloaded on location is by using the simple rule of thumb that 100 watts equals 1 amp. The actual formula is amps = watts/volts. This formula will help you calculate an actual situation. If you do not want to figure it out, Table 8.1 shows common lamp wattages and typical voltages found on location.

Table 8.1: *Watts vs. Voltages*

Load (watts)	Line Current Voltage (amps)			
	110	115	117	120
50	0.5	0.4	0.4	0.4
100	0.9	0.9	0.9	0.8
200	1.8	1.7	1.7	1.7
250	2.3	2.2	2.1	2.1
500	4.5	4.3	4.3	4.2
650	5.9	5.6	5.5	5.4
750	6.8	6.5	6.4	6.2
1000	9.0	8.7	8.5	8.3
1500	13.6	13.0	12.8	12.5
2000	18.1	17.4	17.1	16.7
4000	36.4	34.8	34.2	33.3
5000	45.4	43.5	42.7	41.7
7000	63.6	60.8	59.8	58.3
10,000	90.0	86.9	85.5	83.3

If you determine that there is not enough power at available outlets, take a picture of the breaker box with the front panel removed so you will know the correct type of clip locks to get for your tie-in. (We will discuss proper tie-in procedure in Chapter 9.) Measure the length of cable runs to your shooting site and obtain permission to string cables through hallways or adjoining rooms. Always note the names and phone numbers of those who grant permission so they can be reached for confirmation if you run into problems later on. Take no one's word for anything! If someone tells you, "I think the breakers for those outlets are in that closet," do not believe them. Check it out for yourself. When you set up, are ready to shoot, and a breaker kicks, you should not waste time trying to find out where control for that circuit is located and who has the key for the closet in which the service panel is located. Confirm all of these things at the time of your survey. Often times, the nearest service panel is not the one that controls your area, and house electricians may not know where to find the correct panel without causing lengthy delays.

Ask what activities might be going on during your scheduled shooting times. Just because the area is quiet during the time of your survey, do not assume that that will be the case on the day of shooting. You may be coming in on Saturday when the carpets are shampooed, the floors buffed, or a new wall is being installed in the room next door. If construction is scheduled or other noisy activity is likely to take place, see what can be arranged. You may have to change your shooting schedule.

Make note of special problem areas. Large, shiny surfaces, furniture or plants that may not be appropriate to your production, distracting wall hangings, or other items that you want removed or changed in dressing the set properly should be noted. Get permission to make changes, if possible. See if you can bring in other furniture or artwork from surrounding offices or areas. If so, look at the items during your survey and begin the necessary paperwork to have them on set when you arrive to shoot. If the necessary items are not available inhouse, you will have to bring them with you. Always replace borrowed items when you have finished with them.

Inquire about methods of triggering fire alarms or sprinkler systems. If the ceiling contains heat sensors and you place a bounce light near one, you may make many enemies and cause extensive damage. Once I was shooting some news footage of a computer demo at a large bank. All the bank executives were clustered around in their pinstriped suits as the computer sales representative extolled the virtues of the hardware. Suddenly the room was flooded with water from the sprinkler system and silent alarms were sent to three fire stations by heat sensors hidden in the ceiling. The heat generated by the computer, the news camera lights, and more bodies in the room than usual had triggered the pandemonium.

Many of these points deal with the challenges posed by newer high-rise buildings. Older buildings and private homes pose their own challenges, the most frequent being insufficient power. As I mentioned earlier, unlike newer structures that usually have circuit breakers in the entrance panels, older buildings are apt to have fuses rather than circuit breakers. Checking the fuse rating and type is often not an accurate indication of circuit capacity. This is because people frequently substitute larger-capacity fuses in those panels when increasing power demands cause fuses to blow frequently. It is not uncommon to find 20-amp fuses on circuits designed for 15-amp operation. I have even found 30-amp fuses on such circuits. During the site survey, you should check the wire size leaving the individual fuse holders. If the size is not stamped on the wire covering, you can determine it by using an inexpensive wire gauge, which is available from any electrical supply house. Table 8.2 shows the ampere capacity for various wire sizes.

The most common of the old fuse type is the plug fuse. It is made in ratings of up to 30 amps. Plug fuses are screwed into the same type of socket that is used in household lamps and ceiling fixtures. A glass or mica window permits you to see if the fuse has blown or not. They are used on the individual branch circuits and are frequently oversized for the wire size of the circuit they are intended to protect.

Rather than carry around dozens of 15- and 20-amp plug fuses to keep location equipment operational, you can purchase a few plug breakers that screw into these sockets. They have a small pin in the center that pops out if the circuit they are protecting is overloaded. To reactivate the circuit, remove some of the load and push the pin back in again. You do not have to replace the unit as you do an ordinary plug fuse.

Table 8.2: *Wire-Size Capacity (Amps)*

No. 14	15
No. 12	20
No. 10	30
No. 8	40
No. 6	55
No. 4	70

Fustats may also be used on branch circuits. They are designed to overcome the problem of using overrated fuses. Though they look similar to plug fuses, their screw bases have different-sized threads for different ampere ratings. It is less likely that fustats will be overrated, but it is possible, since they screw into an adapter that fits the standard plug fuse socket. That adapter may have been improperly sized when it was first installed, so check wire sizes leading from these sockets also. When you know the proper fuse types and ratings, determined by the wire size, take notes and be sure to have proper replacements on hand during the shooting schedule.

In older homes, the mains may also be fused with plug fuses, but cartridge (cylindrical) fuses are probably used. These fuses look like shotgun shells and are held in place by brass contacts that fit snugly around each end of the cartridge. If you are in an older industrial plant, this type of fuse may also be used for branch circuits. Take along a fuse puller in your gadget bag to change this type of fuse. The fuse puller is a non-metallic pliers-type tool that will allow you to safely reach into the entrance panel and pull out cartridge fuses. It is dangerous to use metal pliers for this purpose, since you may touch live contacts that could cause severe electrical shock. Unlike plug-type fuses, cartridge fuses must be removed from the circuit and checked with a continuity tester or ohmmeter to determine if they are blown or not. Visual inspection will not always tell you if it has blown.

Note whether or not the wall outlets are three-wire or two-wire. If they are non-grounded, two-wire outlets, you will want to have plenty of converters on hand during the shoot, as your instruments are certain to have grounded plugs. Never break the ground pin off your instrument plugs to accommodate ungrounded outlets!

If your survey indicates that not even a tie-in will yield enough power to support your shoot, your most convenient and economical solution is to request a temporary drop from the local utility company. See Chapter 9 for more information about temporary drops.

Chapter 9

Location Lighting

Battling the Elements

Exterior Daylight Scenes

In earlier chapters, we dealt with sunlight and its effect on indoor locations. Locations that may be lit by one or more different incandescent, fluorescent, or vapor discharge lamps may also contain large or small window areas that add yet another color temperature to the mix. You will recall that it is necessary to decide which source is the most dominant. Make that your standard, and then color-correct all other sources to it. When you shoot outside during the day, there is little question about the dominant source or what the standard will be. The problem is that the sun is a tough act to follow or even keep up with.

There is a tendency to characterize daylight as 5600°K and to set the camera filter to that position before performing the white balance. However, Table 1.1 shows that the color temperature of daylight ranges from 2000°K to 5600°K. This wide range of color temperature and the different qualities of light produced by the sun's interaction with the earth's atmosphere and surrounding structures provide you with the opportunity to get just the look you want. The trick is to be patient enough to wait for optimum conditions and fast enough to get the shot or shots needed before conditions change. When the sun is your primary source and it's not the color temperature or quality of light you would like, you can do a lot to modify it for narrow- and medium-angle shots. The extremely wide-angle shot will require greater patience for nature to get it right or a greater budget to assist nature.

Often, the attitude that good illumination is good lighting comes into play on exterior daytime locations. Having enough light to keep the engineer happy does not mean the scene is well lit.

In fact, unless it is a very overcast day, chances are that you are dealing with excessive contrast for the video system and have highlights the system cannot handle. You are also likely to have shadows that contain little or no detail. You can begin to solve these problems by using a neutral density (ND) filter pack on the front element of your lens. It will reduce the excessive highlights and allow you to work at a larger f-stop. Once your NDs are in place, you can begin to control the lighting even further.

It is an unfortunate fact of life that if your script calls for many long shots, you will need some pretty high-power equipment to deal with specular lighting on exterior locations. You will need generators, powerful lights, and a sizable budget to pay for the large crew necessary to light properly. The assumption behind this text is that you are not dealing with a major motion picture production, so we will not deal with the needs of such costly projects. What we will address is your ability to provide fill and control source levels for medium shots and close-ups.

Often, when you need an exterior wide shot, you have to concentrate on lighting only a small area of that shot. Usually, some action in the foreground needs attention. Regardless of how confined the area requiring attention may be, you still need some powerful lights and large sheets of diffusion material to temper nature. You are either operating at an extremely small f-stop or are using ND filters to reduce your depth of field. In either case, it will take a great deal of supplemental light to get the job done.

Other than using a camera-mounted Frezzi to fill in some shadows on the face of a news reporter doing a stand-up, television shooters tend to take what nature provides and call it fine. There is no need to settle for "what you see is what you get," but you will need some different equipment than that required for shooting indoors. If your camera has black stretch, an electronic circuit designed to bring out details in heavy shadows, this can be a big help on outdoor shoots, but additional lighting will still be necessary for good control over the look of your shot.

If you do not shoot outdoors often, you can rent what you need for those few occasions.

If you find yourself shooting outdoors in daylight frequently, you may want to invest in some of the equipment necessary to do the job properly. Many reflectors that are used outdoors are also valuable tools for indoor setups; so some of these smaller items will be a good investment, whether you shoot outdoors frequently or not.

Controlling Sunlight

The sun can serve as your backlight or key, depending on how you position the talent. Your job is to provide fill (or key and fill) as needed. To some extent, you can also control the intensity and quality of the sun itself.

The quality and intensity of sunlight can be controlled over an area large enough for medium shots and close-ups using a butterfly or overhead (see Figure 3.1). This is nothing more than a large, up to 30 × 30-foot, lightweight metal frame over which is stretched a lighting control material such as a diffusion silk. These frames can be supported by two or four legs, or can be hung overhead by wires attached to other structures or equipment at the location site. The choice of material can affect both the quality and quantity of the sunlight that reaches the talent. While all material suspended overhead, scrim or silk, will reduce the intensity of the sun, some materials will also diffuse as well as alter color temperature so you can get the warm, soft look you want. Hollywood often uses these when shooting outdoors to soften the light.

Butterflys also reduce the amount of bounce or fill needed to establish desired lighting and exposure ratios. These units are not difficult to set up, but they can be difficult to keep up. Because of their large surface area, they pose a considerable anchorage problem if there is more than a slight breeze. Have plenty of sandbags available to weight down their stands, and be sure to keep a close eye on the weather conditions.

On a video commercial shoot on the beach, I had to deal with an overactive sun. I set up a 6 × 8 butterfly directly over the sofa on the sand (doesn't everyone shoot furniture commercials on the beach?) (see Figure 9.1). Note in Figure 9.2 how the butterfly shades the model. The silk softened the light over the sofa and the model sitting on it. But the wind . . . the butterfly stand was sandbagged (we had plenty of sand), but the wind was making a sail out of the silk. Even with people standing directly on the Matthews stand, the butterfly wanted to become airborne. We just

Figure 9.1: *A little sun on the beach with furniture (unsilked).*

Figure 9.3: *A flexfill on location.*

The extent to which you choose to use reflectors should be based on the look you desire and the amount of current available. Remember that they have many uses for interior shots as well as exterior locations.

How Buildings Effect Shots

In the same way that reflector boards can influence the color temperature of the light they reflect on a scene, so can buildings and other large structures such as semitrailers or billboards. If you have ever toured the backlot of a motion picture studio, you may have noticed that most of the buildings, sound stages, carpentry shops, etc., are painted tan. This is to prevent the large buildings from reflecting light with strange color temperatures onto the exterior sets that are located on the studio property. Actual sets on the backlot are painted with realistic colors, but surrounding structures are kept neutral to prevent color temperature contamination of reflected light. Because buildings and areas of open sky or patches of cloud cover can influence the color temperature of daylight to a large extent, you should perform camera white balance often when shooting outdoors. I suggest that you white balance at least every half hour if the camera remains in the same position (more frequently in early morning or late afternoon). White-balance each time the camera changes position, regardless of how soon it has been since your last white balance. You can never "over—white-balance," but you can do the opposite.

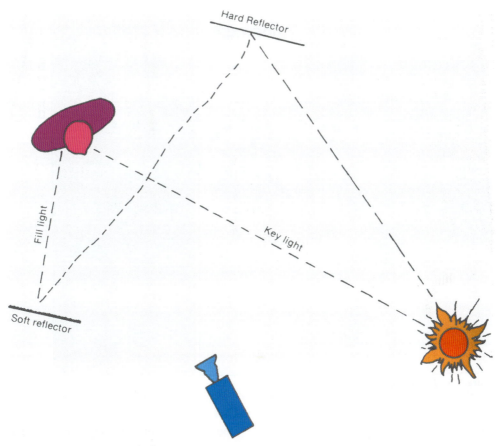

Figure 9.4: *A combination of reflectors.*

In Figure 9.5, two people are standing in front of a building, carrying on a conversation. Actor A is facing the building. Actor B has his back to it. You might be amazed at the difference in color temperature of the light falling on the faces of these two people at any given moment. Assume you are going to shoot a master two-shot from camera position 1, a close-up of actor A from camera position 2, and a reversal medium shot of actors A and B from camera position 3.

Here are the actual color temperature readings taken at the scene in a span of less than 30 seconds. The first reading is taken with the color temperature meter in position X, facing camera position 1. The second reading is taken at Y, facing camera position 2. The third reading places the meter at Z, facing camera position 3. First reading is 5200°K, second reading, 4950°K, and third reading, 5400°K. The difference in color temperature reading is caused by a number of environmental factors. Things such as open sky, clouds, and building surfaces influence reflected light, as does the color of the surface under foot, i.e., concrete, asphalt, sand, grass, etc. Since such variations in color temperature exist, it is wise for you to conduct a white balance procedure each time the camera is moved to shoot in a different direction, regardless of how recent your last white balance

In my film school days, I experimented with shooting day for night. Many movies I studied were obviously shot day for night—people were casting weird shadows, and car headlights just never looked right. In black-and-white film, a red filter and underexposure is used to simulate day for night. However, unless you're shooting a horror film, the red filter makes flesh tones too pale. Day for night just doesn't look convincing.

With modern video cameras it doesn't make sense to try to recreate night unless you are unable to shoot at night. Night shots may be supplemented with artificial lighting to create the exact mood you desire. Wide exterior shots sometime require no additional light (but that's not the purpose of this section). Whether you are dealing with moonlight or multiple artificial sources as your supposed source of illumination, your setup must take its cue from the actual source and must be consistent with the natural look of existing lighting in order to be convincing.

The moon, like the sun, provides light from only one direction. For some reason, moonlight scenes are often lit from a variety of directions. Perhaps this is done on the theory that no one will notice because it is so dark. I notice because, among other flaws, often it is not dark enough. The problem faced is the exact opposite of the one in exterior daylight scenes in which there is often too much light. For night scenes, you must provide a base level sufficient to satisfy the circuit requirements of the camera. Beyond that are the artistic considerations of the scene. Fortunately, current cameras and film stocks are sensitive enough to produce good pictures without requiring light levels that are unconvincingly bright for night scenes (or ones that are too blue to simulate night). With video cameras shooting in light as low as 1 lux, almost no light is needed to create an image.

Whether the scene is supposed to take place under conditions lit by moonlight only or by a combination of moonlight and artificial light sources, there is less need to be concerned about normal color temperature. The concern should be how to achieve a convincing result. We do not expect to see perfect flesh tones in moonlight or under a variety of nighttime exterior light sources.

In Figure 9.7, I had to capture a romantic, moonlit beach in the Caribbean. The moon was the key source of illumination, with the fill being provided by the surface of the sand and water. The color temperature reading was close to 8000°K extremely blue. I white-balanced and achieved a realistic shot. If people were to be walking on the beach, I would have had to add supplemental lighting because their faces would have been too dark. Luckily, the camera was able to expose an actual moonlight scene with 5 foot-candles of illumination. Sometimes it's better to let God provide the lighting rather than create it yourself.

In Figure 9.8, the actors walk along the sidewalk from screen left to the gate, open it, and go up the steps onto the porch. They stand by the front door for a moment and talk before crossing to the swing on the screen right end of the porch, where they sit and talk for the remainder of the scene.

From position 1, the camera follows the action as a two-shot from the sidewalk, through the gate, and up to the front door. Then we cut to a close-up of actor B from camera position 2, followed

Figure 9.7: *Moonlight in the Caribbean.*

be projected on the acting areas. If the shades are partially closed, actors can move from areas of colored wash or darkness into areas of different color, with lace patterns adding light and texture to the scene.

From this one simple example you should be able to see how a variety of different looks can be achieved. Whatever combination of effects you desire, it is important to plan early with set designs and dressings to achieve maximal effect through lighting. Consistency and attention to detail will make the difference between creative, convincing results, and conflicting, unbelievable attempts.

If shooting deep in the woods at night, an HMI is an excellent source of light to simulate moonlight. HMIs give off a very white light on video and this looks more natural than the deep blue commonly used for moonlight. If the daylight-balanced HMI (5600°K) is used and the camera is white balanced for tungsten, you have your slightly blue light. The trees will cast long, deep shadows exactly the way the real full moon does.

One brief note on white balancing scenes such as this. If you have all your lights in their positions and gelled, you may think that it's time to do a white balance. If you did, the camera would not recognize the blue light as a desired effect, but it would average all the colors available. In situations where you want a specific type of colored light to be prominent, it's best to white-balance before the colored gels are added. Use this as a rule of thumb. Once the white balance has been set, any colored light will remain that color.

You may also ask which type of filter to use when white balancing night exteriors. Use the filter position that most closely matches your light source. If most of the lights (ungelled) are tungsten, then use that setting. If the moon really is your key, use the daylight balance. You will get an entirely different look if you white-balance using the "wrong" filter. Look at a color monitor and see the difference balancing on each filter makes, then choose the setting you prefer.

May the Force be with You

Adequate power is the force I am talking about, and let's face it: Most of the time it is not with you. When you get into any situation that involves more than simple three-point lighting of a static head shot, chances are that the power available will not be adequate. When that is the case, you have one of three choices for interior shooting. You can rent a generator and its associated distribution equipment, a costly solution that may be necessary if the project is an ambitious one. You may be able to get by with installing a tie-in to the existing service entrance panel, or you can phone the new business division of your electric utility company and request the installation of a temporary service drop at the location site.

A request should be made 1 to 2 weeks before the scheduled shoot date, and you will have to install your own bull switch or breaker box, following local codes, at the site before they bring power to it. The cost for such a service ranges from about $250 for locations that are fed by underground feeds to $500 for sites requiring an aerial or overhead drop. For that fee they will provide you with 100 to 200 amps of current and a meter of your own. You will have to pay for the current used plus the initial installation fee. Though this method is technically not a tie-in, it uses the same basic hardware as a tie-in but provides more power than would otherwise be available and removes the possible hazard involved in connecting your leads to an existing service entrance.

However, you do need the necessary lead time and the cost for the installation fee.

A generator or temporary service drop will provide more power at the location than would be available from a tie-in. The tie-in does not make additional power available, it merely makes it possible for you to get maximum use of unused power in a very convenient manner. If the service entrance panel is rated at 200 amps, that is the maximum amperage available for the combined use of your needs and the normal, necessary power requirements of the location. If there are computers, air conditioning, or refrigeration units, etc. that must remain on during your shooting schedule, you have to subtract their consumption from the 200-amp total in order to determine the remainder available for your use. Generator setups and temporary service drops bypass the normal power requirements of a site and allow you full use of whatever current capacity they provide.

Tie-Ins

If you determine that there is not enough current available at the outlets located in the vicinity of your set but that there is sufficient unused power available at the entrance panel for your needs, you should plan for a tie-in. That will make it possible for you to distribute all the power not required by the normal needs of the location directly to your area. You will bypass house wiring, eliminate voltage drops, and give yourself more complete and readily accessible control of the circuits you are using.

Tie-in Equipment

You may not own the proper equipment necessary to complete a tie-in, but it is readily available from any major lighting rental facility. The cost for such equipment ranges anywhere from about $300 to $500 per day, depending on the extent of distribution required and your location. This cost is less than that for renting a generator and will pay for itself in speedier setups and strikes as well as eliminate delays caused by blown breakers or fuses during shooting.

The following information regarding tie-ins is not intended to encourage you to attempt making a tie-in if you do not have a basic knowledge of electricity or have a general fear of electricity. That fear could keep you out of serious trouble. It is best to leave tie-ins to a professional electrician if you have any doubt about the techniques or equipment involved.

Installing a Tie-in

Installing a tie-in is not difficult, but care should always be taken when you are working with electricity to avoid fire or personal injury. The greatest hazard exists at the time you connect the clips to the service entrance bus bars. Be sure to wear insulated rubber gloves and to stand on a dry, nonconductive surface. The gloves should be handled carefully to prevent any punctures from occurring. A pinhole in a set of rubber gloves will render them useless as insulators between your body and the current present in the service panel.

The equipment required for a tie-in is not expensive, and only the best should be used. A tie-in is no place to cut corners. Do not try to use ordinary alligator clips to fasten your cables to the buses of the service entrance panel. Use only approved clips that screw tightly to the current source and provide adequate insulation. After they are attached, be sure to secure them with dry ropes to some solid item to prevent their being pulled loose or being brought into contact with other legs or a ground by accident. Your first connection should always be to the ground bus of the service entrance. The other end of this connection should be securely fastened to a known earth ground such as a cold water pipe or a brass rod that you have driven into the ground to a depth of at least 3 feet.

The next connection should be made to the neutral wire of the entrance bus. Your final connections should be made to the hot bus or buses of the panel, taking great care not to short two hots together or short a hot to a neutral or ground. You can place a piece of heavy rubber or fiberboard between the two hot clips to prevent accidental shorting.

The secured leads from the service entrance panel are then connected to your own breaker panel, commonly called a "bull switch," taking care to keep the polarity straight throughout your distribution system.

It's important that your bull switch not only have a master breaker and disconnect switch for emergency shutoff of your entire distribution system, but that each branch have its own breaker for selective shutdown of circuits as a way of preventing a short on any one branch from taking your whole system down.

From the branch breakers of the bull switch, power can be distributed by two methods:

1. You can use 15-, 20-, 30- or 50-amp female twistlock connectors that are mounted in power strips on the same board as the bull switch. Distribution cables with the appropriate male twistlock plugs on one end and stage boxes on the other can be used for further distribution before being converted to Edison plugs using a 1900 box.
2. Distribution cables with twistlock plugs on one end can be terminated on the other end directly with 1900 boxes. This is really a matter of personal preference, tempered by the necessary cable lengths needed to get from the service entrance to the location site.

In most cases, if you need to bring large amounts of current from the butt switch to the location site over long distances, you will be better off using welder's cable for each leg and neutral rather than more expensive heavy-duty three- or four-conductor cable. Such multiconductor cable is extremely heavy and bulky to transport and is incapable of handling the large loads that can be readily handled by individual strands of welder's cable. Welder's cable is generally terminated on each end with a male or female Mole-pin connector.

Chapter 10
Studio Lighting
The Good Life

The studio environment offers many advantages over location work. It represents the good life because it has sufficient power, a rigging system of some type to hang instruments from, and probably a power distribution arrangement with a dimming control package. In addition, air conditioning will keep you from melting during repeated takes. For all of its comforts, the studio still poses a problem you do not face on location. How do you create the illusion that the background for an exterior scene has the expanse that occurs in nature? How do you create natural-looking exteriors outside windows and doors of studio sets or create the illusion of infinite space?

There are two basic approaches to these problems. The first solution is to use a large neutral background known as a "cyclorama," or "cyc." The second method is to use electronic devices such as chroma key, Newsmatte, Ultimatte, or create a Virtual Set, which may be used in conjunction with a good cyc. All of these approaches have special lighting requirements that must be taken into consideration. The degree of success you achieve with these methods is directly proportional to the care you take with the lighting. The better the lighting, the more convincing the end results will be.

Cycloramas

One of the most versatile and valuable assets of any studio is a good cyc setup. However, it places high demands on power and air conditioning requirements, and must be connected to a dimming stem to be truly effective. There are two basic types of cycs: hard and soft.

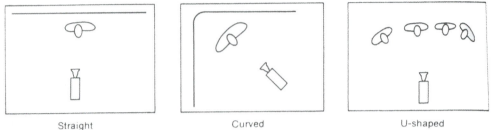

| Straight | Curved | U-shaped |

Figure 10.1: *Basic cyc shapes.*

When cycs are constructed using a variety of solid materials such as concrete, lath, and plaster or plasterboard, they are referred to as "hard cycs." Usually, however, cycs are made of fabric stretched over a frame to form a smooth surface and are called "soft cycs." Each type has its own advantages and can be configured in any of the three basic shapes, as shown in Figure 10.1.

Hard Cycs

The simplest form of a hard cyc is illustrated on the left in Figure 10.2. It is a plain plaster wall with cyc strips mounted about 8 feet in front of its surface at the top. The simple straight wall arrangement has a separate, movable, ground row sweep that is placed at the base to help create the illusion of infinity and make it more difficult to detect where the wall meets the floor. A "sweep" is a curved masking piece that sweeps up from the horizontal surface toward the cyc or back wall (see the illustration left of center in Figure 10.2). However, such an arrangement will not equal the effectiveness of a cyc that has an integrated sweep like that shown right of center in Figure 10.2. It is the most expensive form of cyc and blends the wall with the floor in a gradual integrated sweep. These hard cycs, with a built-in sweep, create the most convincing illusion of infinity. If the cyc is higher than 12 feet, it will probably require light from below as well as above to be lit evenly. In such cases, the ground row sweeps can be moved forward and lighting instruments can be placed behind them as illustrated on the far right in Figure 10.2.

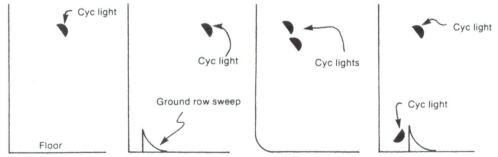

Figure 10.2: *Basic cyc designs.*

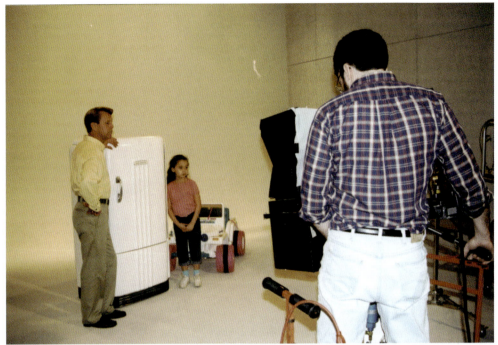

Figure 10.3: *Cyc with talent.*

Figure 10.3 shows an example of a curved cyc. Note the bend in the wall behind the talent. In Figure 10.4, the curve in the wall appears much more pronounced; it is the same set as in Figure 10.3, but the telephoto lens gives you a better idea of the angle of the curve. In Figure 10.5, the curve on the wall seems to disappear when viewed straight on.

In more expensive installations, if the cyc is more than 12 feet high and requires additional lighting from the bottom to achieve an even wash, a trench may be created in the floor to conceal the strips rather than using a ground row sweep (see Figure 10.6). As the contour of the cyc increases in complexity from a straight line design to a curve or U-shape, the costs rise accordingly, especially when an integrated curved sweep is formed to join the cyc with the floor.

Soft Cycs

If the cyc is constructed of fabric, there are a number of ways to approach the situation, and some of them are quite sophisticated. In the simplest case, a large, seamless piece of muslin or canvas can be stretched with grommets and tie lines between an upper and lower batten, and vertical battens on either end. Again, as with hard cycs, if the surface is over 12 feet high, it will be necessary to light it from the bottom as well as the top to obtain an even wash of sufficient intensity in deep colors. This can be accomplished by hiding the lower lighting instruments with a ground row or sweep, or by creating a trench in the studio floor to conceal the instruments. These methods of concealment will work with a straight, curved, or U-shaped arrangement.

Figure 10.4: *Straight cyc (note curve on wall).*

Figure 10.5: *Straight cyc.*

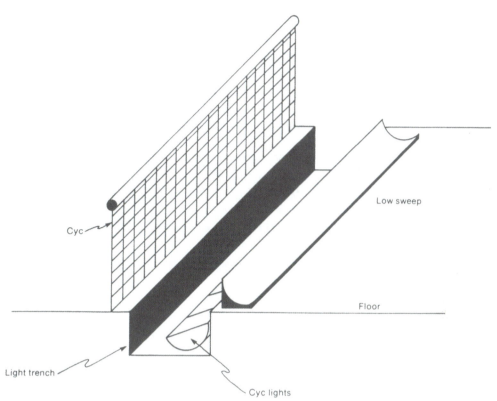

Figure 10.6: *Trench cyc.*

A great variety of effects can be created with multiple-layer fabric cycs using nothing more than close control of the light on each layer of fabric. Although multiple-layer cycs have traditionally called for a hefty investment in instrumentation, power, space, and air conditioning requirements, newer instrumentation and cyc materials available today make the same effects possible with fewer layers and less consumption.

While a single layer of material is adequate in many situations, the multi-layer approach is often used when many different effects have to be made on a real-time basis during performances of musical numbers or within a dramatic scene. Such effects might involve changing the background from a bright blue sky with white clouds to a stunning sunset and on to a star-filled evening sky.

The type of cyc you construct should be based on the needs of your productions. If they require nothing more than a plain neutral sky, install a single-layer blue cyc material that can be lit with white light only. This arrangement requires less expensive, single-circuit cyc lights that use fewer watts, since the light output is not cut by the use of gels, and puts less burden on the air conditioning system.

If you must produce minimal changes in your backgrounds during production, choose an off-white or gray muslin and light it with a two-circuit arrangement of cyc lights. White muslin or canvas should never be used as cyc material, even if you desire a white background, because once you start with a material that reflects more than 60% of the light that falls on it, you will create a situation in which the actors and scenery placed in front of the cyc will tend to be silhouetted against the bright background. Even if you do not put any light on such a cyc directly, spill from the other lights can create problems.

With a two-circuit cyc lighting system, you can gel the instruments with the two colors needed for the scene and then cross-fade from one to the other, as required, to introduce a change during the scene.

For the greatest flexibility in the creation of effects, a two-layer cyc and a three- or four-circuit cyc light arrangement work best. A natural-color shark's tooth scrim is hung about 1 foot in front of the off-white muslin or canvas backing. This has a twofold advantage over the single-layer cyc. As the light strikes the mesh scrim, it creates a much softer look, which creates a more believable impression of infinity. You can also place small Italian lights on the front surface of the muslin layer. When these lights are turned on, they shine through the open mesh of the scrim and create very believable stars in the evening sky. Since there is bound to be some movement of the scrim in front of the lights, caused by natural drafts in the studio, this movement causes the stars to twinkle in a believable and random fashion as they are alternately exposed to the spaces and solid areas of the shark' s tooth scrim.

Ages ago, CBS used a three-layer cyc in which the third layer was used to create the illusion of clouds in the sky. An opaque black Duvetyne (a black cloth) layer backed up the entire cyc with random cloud-shaped holes cut out and lined with mesh or scrim to maintain their shape. When the scoops or skypans were lit, they projected a soft-edge, cloud-shaped pattern on the muslin, and the effect was further softened by the front layer of scrim. This arrangement of the back layer and its associated backlights required a great deal of backstage space and is not used today because of more efficient special effects projectors such as the Great American Scene Machine covered in Chapter 11. These effects machines achieve even better effects with no sacrifice in precious studio floor space.

Efforts to blend the ground row evenly with the floor and cyc can be handled effectively by using a series of Fresnels aimed directly down on the ground row and controlled by dimmer circuits. This is an effective way to control the intensity of the ground row and achieve the desired results. These Fresnels must be gelled with the same colors used in the main cyc strips. Placement of the cyc strips should be guided by the manufacturer's photometrics to achieve the greatest efficiency. You want an even wash with the greatest output per watt. Generally, this will mean placing the cyc strips 8 to 10 feet in front of the cyc.

Cyc Lighting and Equipment

For the past 30 years, we have had to use pretty much the same type of material and lighting instruments to build functional cycs. Since this older material and equipment is more universally available, we will deal with it in this chapter as we discuss cyc lighting methods and equipment.

During the past couple of years, some new items have been developed that reduce cyc construction costs, space, power, and air conditioning requirements. These newer materials will be discussed in Chapter 11. The concepts and techniques remain pretty much the same, whether new or old technology is involved. Live theater makes frequent and extensive use of cycs. The lighting instruments used usually consist of relatively inexpensive strip-lights or borderlights that have three or four circuits of lamps ranging in size from 100 to 300 watts. The lamps may be R-40s or as simple as conventional household lamps, each in its own separate compartment. This compartment may have a colored, round, glass lens called a "roundel" that covers the opening, or it may be equipped to receive any color gel sandwiched in a gel frame.

A typical three-circuit arrangement may consist of alternate circuits of primary red, blue, and green, and use roundels or gels to color the light. A fourth circuit may add pure white light to the mixture to increase the versatility of effects. Because of the relatively low wattages and heat dispersion involved, permanent glass roundels or inexpensive gel material may be used in front of the lamps. Unfortunately, these instruments do not produce enough intensity to adequately light a television cyc. What looks great to the human eye in the theater will do little to produce an acceptable image for the television camera.

Television cyc lights range from 750 to 2000 watts each and require larger, more expensive instruments and more costly color media, but there has been little choice in these matters until some recent developments that will be covered in Chapter 11.

Newsmatte and Ultimatte

Although chroma key has been improved technically since its introduction in the early 60s, it still has some drawbacks and telltale signs that limit its use when high-quality matting is required. A father and son team, Victor and Paul Vlahos, have invented more sophisticated matting systems. The less costly of the two is Newsmatte, designed for live telecasts involving such things as matting graphics for weather reports, with live studio shots of the weather forecaster. The more costly and sophisticated unit is called Ultimatte. It is intended for critical use in post-production matting to combine live-action foreground material with prerecorded background information. Thanks to a major breakthrough in encoding and decoding techniques, it is even possible to achieve flawless Ultimatte composites using foreground material that has been recorded on any of the digital formats.

In addition, many news sets are going the route of virtual reality or virtual sets. In a virtual set, nothing exists except the talent and a cyc or background. When combined in the virtual system, the computer removes the phony background and the talent now walks around a set that is completely computer-generated.

For fans of the old TV series *Star Trek: The Next Generation* the Holodeck was an example of a virtual set or environment. Just as the weather forecaster looks at a monitor to tell where he or she is pointing on the map, the talent will only see the completed set they are in when looking at the monitor. After the initial investment in the virtual system, a substantial cost savings can be realized because new sets do not have to be built—they are simply created in the computer and layered into the video.

Composite Lighting

Realistic lighting of the foreground is as important as anything else in making the composite look natural and realistic. Again, the key light must come from the same direction as the light in the background scene, but it is just as important that the contrast ratio of the foreground lighting match that of the background. If the background material has flat lighting, then so must the foreground elements.

TV stations and post houses that still use chroma key have to make sure their lighting is exact. The switcher removes everything it sees of a particular color saturation and hue. Most places use either chroma key blue or green. These colors were selected because they are unique enough to not appear in most fabrics, set props, or people.

Everything that exists in that deep color saturation and specific hue disappears. A background, generated by another source, replaces the blue or green. This presents a few problems.

If the talent is wearing anything that matches the blue or green, it too will disappear when keyed. Often, people with blue eyes had to get tinted contact lenses that wouldn't "key out." Orphan Annies don't go over well on television.

Lighting is also extremely important. It must be flat. If too much shadow is thrown on the chroma key background, that will make it darker and harder to key. Everything must remain even. Back-lighting is not as critical in this type of setup because the background will be eliminated.

The switcher operator on a live broadcast or the NLE operator on a taped event must adjust the clip until the background color disappears and the desired background is in its place. Hairstyles used to be a problem because the fine ends and frizzies would leave traces of electronic noise and pulsate wildly. Most of the newer equipment has eliminated this problem and leaves sharp, clean edges (see Figure 10.7).

The way to achieve the best matting is by using Stewart Ultimatte blue screen material for the background screen, because it provides the greatest separation between the blue and green spectrums. If it is not available or your budget does not permit its use, there are two approved sources for Ultimatte blue paint. They are Rosco and Gothic Color. Of the two paints, the Gothic Ultimatte blue comes closest to the blue-green separation provided by the Stewart Ultimatte blue screen material (see the Appendix). If the background element was an exterior scene, the easiest

Figure 10.7: *Chroma key at work.*

method to achieve a convincing composite is to shoot the blue screen outside in the parking lot or up on the roof. The easiest way to match sunlight is to use sunlight. It is the best way to get a match between exterior background material and foreground subjects that are to look as though they were a part of the original background.

When planning a composite, shoot the background material first, and then light the foreground to match. If you light the foreground subject in the studio so that it looks good to the naked eye and then matte it over previously unseen background material, the end result will never be believable.

With the background in the can, the next step is to light the foreground subject to match it. When you go into the studio to complete the composite, light the blue screen after you light the foreground talent or scenic element, especially if you want it to cast a shadow on the background. If you want cast shadows to appear on the background, position your key light so it causes a shadow to fall on the blue screen. Such a setup will result in spill from the key on the blue screen background. If you already lit the blue screen so that it was extremely evenly lit, you would create a problem for yourself. Even though you can see a shadow on the blue screen in the studio, it will not key in because it will be necessary to set the clips on the Ultimatte or Newsmatte to a lower setting to remove the excess light from the key that strikes the background. When you make this adjustment, it will bring the level of the cast shadow even with the normal background level of the blue screen, and the shadow will disappear from the final composite (see Figure 10.8).

A

B

Figure 10.8: *Ultimatte.*

Convincing Matting

There are two crucial elements involved when lighting foregrounds for convincing matting. They are backlighting and side lighting. Side lighting is particularly crucial because often when you look at someone standing in front of a blue screen, you will notice light bouncing off the screen onto the talent. To the naked eye this looks like good backlight or side lighting. However, when it is properly adjusted, the Ultimatte will remove that blue spill and produce a negative effect on the final composite. Without good white light directed at the subject from the back and the side, once the blue spill is removed, the foreground elements will be surrounded with what looks like a dark shadow in the final composite. You will naturally think the matte is bad. It is not. The electronics are doing precisely what they are designed to do.

The problem is an absence of good white side light. This effect is bothersome when the background material is high key. If, however, the background material is low key or very dark, this absence of sidelight will work in your favor to create a more natural composite. In such a case, side light would only cause an unnatural glow around the edge of the foreground elements. Sidelight sources can be soft or specular in nature, depending on the look you are trying to match. Fresnels might be used when matching the look of a background that was shot outside on a sunny day, but softlights might be appropriate if the background material was shot in a fluorescent-lit office environment or outside on an overcast day.

The use of an amber backlight, like that recommended in some chroma key situations, is not a good idea for Ultimatte. It will only give an amber cast to the foreground subject. It will not create a better matte. The design of the Ultimatte automatically takes care of blue spill without creating a ragged edge around the talent. (Light for Newsmatte or Ultimatte composites as though the foreground subject were situated in front of a black velvet drape. Any spill from the blue screen will not be seen in the final composite. Whatever light you want to see in the finished matte must be put there by you.)

The most important thing about lighting the blue background screen is consistency in terms of evenness and color temperature. If the color temperature of the background screen varies, it will cause a hue shift in the final background scene. For this reason, dimmers cannot be used to even out the illumination of the background screen. The instruments must be moved closer to the screen, or farther back, to adjust for intensity differences. Scrims might also be used, but they provide definite steps rather than gradual degrees of intensity correction. Cyc strips are the easiest instruments to use since they are designed to produce an even wash of light over large areas.

Even lighting is relatively easy to achieve over a limited blue screen area when you are only matting the upper body of talent in the foreground. If the foreground subject must be seen from head to foot, walking down a path for instance, the lighting task becomes far more complicated as you try to achieve even lighting where the blue back wall blends with the blue floor. When you light the floor, do not light it straight down from above, because the light will kick back into the camera as specular white light and destroy the even wash you are trying to create. The use of a

Chapter 11

Future Directions

Watts New?

The majority of items that are new and different in the lighting field involve the application of modern technology to earlier approaches. The end result is generally a smaller, more efficient widget that takes the place of the earlier device. While the first product discussed here is certainly the application of modern technology, I am not aware of any previous device involving the same concept, except for in specialized medical applications.

HMI Offspring: the Fiber-Optic System

A product of the LTM Corporation, the fiber-optic system has an HMI light source and a variety of fiber-optic attachments. It is called the Micro-Set Lighting (MSL) system.

The MSL 250 system consists of two main units and as many as eight attachments that allow you to bend, distribute, and focus the output in a variety of unique ways. Like any HMI source, the system starts with a ballast to convert the AC line current to high-voltage DC. This DC current is then fed to a separate light box that contains a 250-watt HMI daylight lamp and has a port for the attachment of various accessories. The ballast can also be powered by a 12-volt DC supply such as an auto battery.

The attachments include the CML 100 fiber-optic bundle, which contains 100 2.5-foot fiber-optic strands. Each strand is covered with a wear-resistant black sheathing. These strands may be used separately or in bundles. I used this type of lighting in glamour photography and video, where I have very little space for light but still need the output (see Figure 11.1).

Figure 11.1: *Fiber-optic lighting used in a car.*

My initial reaction to this accessory was, "Big deal! What good is it?" Then I started thinking about the many times I was working with tabletop setups and needed a bit of light here or there and had to try to restrict the output of an inky enough so that it did the job without washing out everything else in the display. This product works well for that and other applications. You also have the luxury of using the "poor person's approach" and use small makeup mirrors to reflect the light when you want it to go. But having the source itself, positioned where you desire it, is far better.

The CML 4 contains only four fiber-optic strands of much larger diameter and has two very useful accessories. One is the Microlite, which has a Fresnel and a barn door. It makes an excellent fill inside cars, trucks, and planes because it is extremely small and lightweight and can be mounted in very cramped locations. Since there is no heat at all at the end of the fiber-optic cables (like an LED light), you do not have to worry about scorching autointeriors or roasting the talent. Since the color temperature of the unit is 5600°K, it does not require booster blue gel to match sunlight, and is extremely powerful. It produces 1400 foot-candles for a 2-inch diameter beam at a distance of 1 foot from the subject—more than enough to add fill in bright sunlight. Even if another type of instrument did produce such high output, no human could stand the heat it would generate in close quarters.

This handy Fresnel can be mounted outside the vehicle to shine through side or front windows. It can also be used for many other applications.

The six-light bar attached to a CML 4 fiber-optic shaft is also great for interior vehicle use, clipped to a sun visor for fill or to the dash to simulate instrument lighting for nighttime scenes. Gels and neutral densities (NDs) can be used—in the same way they are used with conventional instruments—to color-correct or reduce the MSL's output.

If you are involved in commercial production and the soap company wants to show its product in the best possible light, this is the device for you. A fiber-optic strand can be placed in the bar of soap to make it shine from within, and because there is no heat, the bar will not melt after the first take. A model submerged in a tub of bubble bath will look very glamorous when the water and bubbles are lit from below. Since there is no current in the fiber-optic strands, they can be submerged in liquids without endangering the talent.

A fiber-optic in a beverage will give it a punch like you have never seen before. Think about it for a minute. There are many times when you need lots of cold light in confined or dangerous locations. Shooting microchips, for instance. Think about the manufacturing equipment, factories, and plants you are called on to light and how difficult it is to do. The MSL system certainly has application for these and many other assignments. The designers at LTM even invite you to challenge them to design an accessory for this system that will solve some extremely difficult lighting situation you are facing.

Since the entire system costs about $6000, it probably will not sell like hot cakes, but a daily rental rate of about $200 puts it within reach of most production budgets.

This may be a glimpse at the future of studio and theater lighting. The time may come when a few large light sources are attached to multiple instruments with fiber-optic cables.

Hollywood has been using fiber optics since their inception. When models are built for films (*Star Trek, Titanic*, etc.) fiber optics are the means by which they are illuminated. Before the development of fiber optics, other more difficult and costly methods have had to be used.

Softlights: Sort Of

The success of the first HMI instruments with Fresnel lens systems proved the technology and the ultimate economy of this power-saving form of illumination. The soft, airy quality of the light was also appreciated by many cinematographers. This led to the development of the Molecool from Mole-Richardson. This light utilizes a new concept that uses 30-, 120-, 220- or 240-volt lamps running on either AC or DC. This easily boosts the daylight levels without generating the heat that HMIs often do (see Figure 11.2). This compact HMI light brings the same power and economy to the set as regular Fresnel instruments do, and it results in a far more efficient unit. It is possible to light a 15-foot-wide area 13 feet high to an intensity of 360 foot-candles at a distance of 10 feet—an impressive coverage when compared with conventional lights. This 1200-watt instrument draws only 10 amps.

Figure 11.2: *1200-Watt Molequartz two light Molecool (Photo courtesy of Mole-Richardson Co.).*

Hard Lights

Just as the HMI softlights have caught on in commercial circles and with lighting directors who are looking for powerful diffuse sources, the hard rock crowd has fallen in love with HMI PARs (see Figure 11.3). These rather harsh (specular) sources lend themselves well to the strong shafts of light that are frequently swiveled around smoke-filled rock stages. This type of PAR light is now being used by network news crews for interior and exterior lighting setups.

Because they are extremely bright 5600°K sources, they can be used as fill in exterior daylight setups or can be bounced off ceilings for interior news coverage to provide a good soft fill for

Figure 11.3: *A 575-Watt HMI Molepar (Photo courtesy of Mole-Richardson Co.).*

"talking head" interviews. A 575-watt PAR 46 can provide 45,000 foot-candles at 10 feet. The lamp life is rated at a minimum of 1000 hours. Like any HMI instrument, a ballast is required, and the Strand Century ballast unit for the 575-watt ParLite weighs 32 pounds.

One of the things I enjoy most when using HMIs in video is how they affect whites. If you point an HMI at a white object, the white almost fluoresces. It actually makes the whites "pop" on a shoot. When shooting exteriors and I really want to impress the client, I'll use HMIs to light the exterior of his or her business.

A 1200 PAR has much more impact and throw than a standard HMI 1200. Because of the wavelength of light produced by the HMI, the whites appear much brighter and more visually striking.

In Figure 11.4, an HMI PAR was used to supplement the sun. Sometimes the sun does not do what you want it to do—that is where HMIs come into play. Detergent commercials always use HMIs to shoot the "whiter whites." Yes, Ultra Glip actually makes your whites whiter—if you point an HMI at them!

The MR-16 Family: the First in a Long Line

In the beginning, there were ordinary tungsten 35 mm projection lamps. They were very hot and required heavy, forced ventilation to prevent slide meltdown. Along came Emmet Wiley, who designed the multimirrored MR-16 lamp. Its unique properties permit the infrared and ultraviolet rays to pass through the efficient reflector bowl rather than projecting them forward with the beam of light. The result is a much cooler beam and brighter slides.

This first MR-16 projection lamp was not suitable for general lighting purposes because of the nature of its secondary focal point. It produced a very uneven field of light when used as a source for open-faced lighting instruments. Then came George Panagiotou, who reasoned that the secondary focal point of the MR-16 could be changed to adapt it to general lighting applications. He spent several years redesigning the lamp so it would produce a more even light field and started marketing his new version of the MR-16 in a portable fixture called the Mini-Cool (see Figure 11.5). Photometrics show the newly designed 250-watt MR-16 lamp produces a higher light output than an ordinary 600-watt lamp. The Mini-Cool led to the development of other similar instruments such as the Anton Bauer single and dual-lamp Ultra Light.

Decasource Lighting

Realization of the potential of such an efficient, compact 3200°K source led to the development of other instrument types. The idea is now being used in miniature versions of a 30-light unit, such as the DecaPod, 2250-watt lighting system from DecaSource (www.decasource.com). These instruments are designed to use either 120-volt lamps in the same manner as their larger counterparts or 12-volt lamps in series, much like the mini-strips described later in the chapter. Thirty

Figure 11.4: *An HMI PAR on location.*

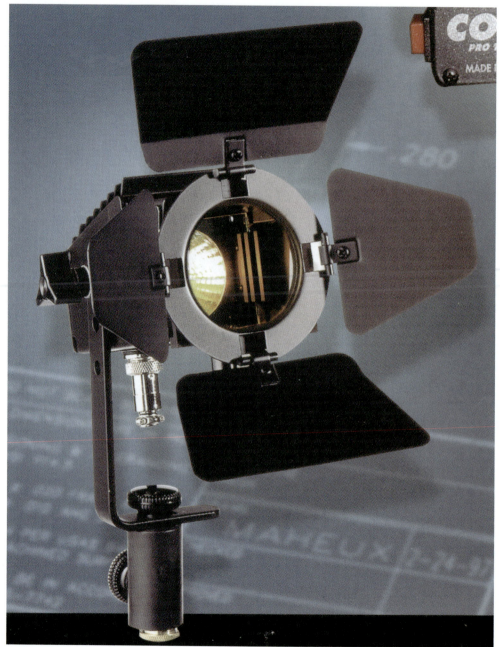

Figure 11.5: *Cool-Lux Mini-Cool (Photo courtesy of Cool-Lux, Inc.).*

75-watt MR-16 lamps on three circuits producing 2250 watts was designed for intense light output without the intense heat (see Figure 11.6). At a distance of 10 feet, 1300 foot-candles is output with a narrow 12-inch beam. If more output is desired, a 150-light, 11250-watt PentaLight, or a 300-light, 22500-watt DecaLight should suffice.

Mini-Strips

When Jules Fisher decided to take one of his shows on the road many years ago, a problem arose when the wagons were redesigned with a lower profile than those used in the Broadway production. Those higher wagons had concealed conventional theatrical strip-lights that washed a cyc. The new wagons would not hide the necessary strips. Mr. Fisher called on Victor En Yu Tan to work out a solution. What resulted was the low-voltage Mini-Striplight that uses ten MR-16 lamps per circuit, wired in series (see Figure 11.7). A neon indicator was designed to indicate which lamp had blown, since the series arrangement caused all lamps in the circuit to go out. These remarkably compact striplights, manufactured by both Strand Lighting and Lighting & Electronics, Inc., are extremely powerful and offer a viable alternative to conventional cyc lights on location. Theatrical striplights will not do the job, and legitimate cyc lights are very difficult to rent. These charmers will get the job done, and they are beginning to appear at rental houses around the country. They are also good for providing floods and washes in hallways and other confined locations. They can be easily fastened to a ceiling or concealed behind a small false beam.

Mini-Fresnels

The first application of the MR-16 lamp to a line of compact Fresnel instruments was undertaken by Lighting & Electronics, Inc. The 4.5-inch, 250-watt ENH MR-16 lamp Mini-Fresnel provides light output equal to a standard 6-inch 750-watt Fresnel. At the moment, the manufacturer does not recommend using this lamp under conditions where it might be bumped during operation, because it blows out rather easily when vibrated. Designers are working to produce a hardier version of the lamp. With the exception of this problem, it is a great little instrument. These Fresnels also come in 150-, 250- and 300-watt sizes.

Research is under way by the people at Cool-Lux to manufacture an MR-16-type lamp with a replaceable lamp capsule. This would substantially reduce the cost of lamp replacement, since the most costly part of the current lamp is the specially coated multifaceted reflector bowl.

The MR-16 lamp, like the earlier quartz-halogen lamp, makes possible the design of even more efficient and compact instruments to help you place shadows more precisely in your scenes. Like modern electronic gear, lighting tools are being improved and miniaturized.

Nifty New Products

These next few items are not as innovative as the previous ones, but they are examples of manufacturers recognizing the needs of professionals, and packaging products that meet those needs.

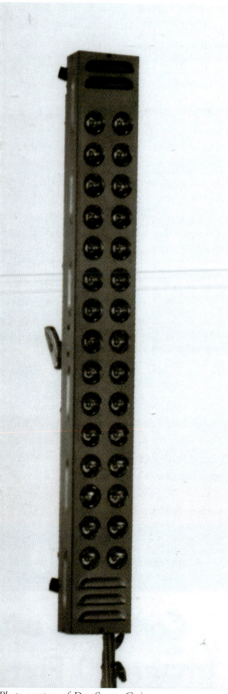

Figure 11.6: *DecaPod light (Photo courtesy of DecaSource Co.).*

Figure 11.7: *Mini-Strips (Photo courtesy of Lighting & Electronics, Inc.).*

I call them "duck feet," but the Matthews people who invented them call them Griff Clips. These interlocking wedge-shaped pieces are designed to allow the hanging of any fabric or diffusion material without damage to the material or the need for tools. One section of the wedge is placed on one side of the material to be hung, and the other section is placed on the opposite side of the fabric and inserted into the wide end of the first section. A ring in the first section can then be attached to suspension ropes. As tension is applied to the ropes, the interlocking wedges tighten and hold the fabric securely without ripping it. Originally intended to hang Griffolyn and other Matthews diffusion textiles used in butterflys or overheads, the Griff Clip can be used for many other fabric or diffusion hanging applications.

If you have done any lighting at all, there has probably been more than one occasion where you used household aluminum foil to mask spill from an instrument or create a snoot or a flag. The problem with ordinary aluminum foil is that it chars under the extremely high heat of an instrument and reflects objectionable spill in a variety of places around the set. While heavy-duty roasting foil does not char under high heat, it does produce unwanted reflections. The Great American Market has been producing a product called Blackwrap, which has a matte black finish and will stand up to the heat of lighting instruments (see Figure 13.3). It is packaged like ordinary household foil. A similar product, called Cinefoil, is manufactured by Rosco. Cinefoil also comes in a Satin Silver version, which reflects light softly and evenly.

The need to adjust intensity on some instruments, such as backlights, effect lights, and background lights, for which exact color temperature is not important, can be easily accomplished with a dimmer. Usually, you would not carry a dimming system around on location but would resort to the use of scrims, which diffuse the light, or ND material, which maintains the specular nature of a source. That means that intensity adjustments require moving the instrument farther away, or replacing or exchanging the scrim or ND.

The use of scrims will only permit corrections in half- or full-stop increments. The first convenient solution I found for such intensity correction was the Photo Dimmer by Cool-Lux. This

Figure 11.8: *The DP bounce.*

Figure 11.9: *2x4-inch and diffusion.*

the light source. They were placed side by side. A 6-foot-long piece of 216 diffusion was thumb-tacked to the studs (we didn't even need to use a silk holder or stand because the studs did the trick). The 216 softened the DP's light, but I still had to do something about the top of the silk. That's where ND9 gel comes in handy. The ND9 was tacked to the top 2 feet of the 216. We now had a gradated, diffused source. The ND on the top lowered the ceiling's level by 2½ stops, while the talent received a normal exposure. Once again, I used what I had available and came up with devices that worked for my application. If I ever run into this type of situation again, I'll know exactly what to do (see Figure 11.9).

My goal in this book is to get you to do the same thing. You don't always have to run out and get the newest and most expensive lighting instrument available. Most of the time, you won't have the budget to get that "special" unit. With the limited time and resources available on your shoot, see what you can do with what you have. You may come up with some new, innovative procedure or instrument that will change the way we light something. If you do, contact me so we can split the royalties.

Remember the phrase "Lights, camera, action"? Lights come first for good reason. Without them, the camera and the action are useless.

This is not quite the end of your instruction. It is the beginning of your ongoing effort to light your subjects more effectively. It is a point at which you begin to apply a new understanding of light and technology to the realities of your profession. It is your opportunity to experience the control you hold over the viewer's perception of every scene—to conceal and reveal selectively, to place shadows and light creatively. So let there be light, but not too much light. Remember, God's job was to illuminate, yours is to light. You are now ready to pass "Go" and begin with actual scenarios.

Chapter 12

Specific Lighting Situations

What Should I Do?

You have now come to the point where you should try your hand at lighting some specific scenarios. I tried to make these actual situations a sample of what you might run into in the lighting world because each of these "sets" poses challenges for the lighting director.

Every one of these "problems" is from one of my shoots, and our lighting team created the look we were after with the equipment we had or had rented. I will start with one of the less complicated setups and explain my concept.

The Lone Interviewee

Our first example is lighting someone who will be interviewed on camera. It does not matter if he or she is looking at the camera, at an off-camera interviewer (as was in our case), or is staring at the ceiling. Your goal is to make this individual's office look pleasing, well lit, and like a real office (which it usually is).

To add a few challenges, the person being interviewed is sitting behind a massive, highly reflective, granite-top desk. Directly behind his mahogany desk is a row of untinted windows—allowing the light from outdoors to flood in. You do not want the talent to be backlit, so his face must be properly exposed. Below the windows are mahogany cabinets (to match the desk) lined with photographs of family members. If this were not enough, your talent has hair as white as newly fallen snow.

Figure 12.13: *A wide shot showing the placement of the HMI and 2K Fresnel.*

With all of this strong backlight coming it from outdoors, we needed a sizeable amount of light to provide fill indoors. Because we wanted the sunlight to appear as such, in no way did we want the fill try to approximate competing with the sun. We still needed strong directionality, but a little fill was needed. Using an Arri 1K Fresnel in a softbox enclosure (like a Chimera, but not that brand), we raised the unit to a height of 6 feet and placed it 4 feet from the actor. To keep the color temperature consistent, we inserted a sheet of booster blue on the white fabric front. This would still give us a slight orange cast (see Figure 12.14). We also placed a 2 × 4-foot piece of foam core on a light stand and arm to act as bounce when shooting the close-ups.

When we shot the person outside from the store employee's perspective, we wanted the exterior to overexpose slightly. On a cloudless, sunny, winter day the light outdoors can easily reach f-22. Our interior illumination reached f-11 with the HMI and 2K pounding through the glass, so 2 stops is acceptable (outside was f-22 and inside f-11).

Once again, because the sunlight was so strong, we just needed to fill in the shadows a little, not try to compete. We were able to get the master shot and the close-ups from the interior, but still lacked getting the shot of the employees from the person's point of view outside.

Figure 12.14: *Fill light and a little bounce.*

When we decided to do the exterior-to-interior scene the next day, we had total cloud cover, so our "sun" had to be duplicated. Bringing the gelled HMI indoors and positioning it 15 feet from the talent (set on flood), extending it 8 feet, we had another f-11 day (see Figure 12.15). We had the correct illumination level, but no sunlight streaming through the door—obviously, the shots would not match. To make them match, we used our daylight gelled 2K and put it in the doorway (vestibule) and punched it through the frame and glass. This provided our streaming sunlight, complete with the door frame shadows across the talent.

Since the person outside would be coming inside on that same shot, the employee had to open the glass door for her. When this happened, with the camera positioning, we saw the reflection of the light and stand in the glass door. Tom Landis solved this problem by gaffer taping black cloth to the light stand and I framed the light out on top. Figure 12.16 illustrated what we did.

Our lighting was almost complete. The backlight was needed for the store employees. As the person from outside walked in, the Arri 2K acted as sunlight through the windows for the employees and her backlight. An Arri 650-watt Fresnel (gelled booster blue) was raised 8 feet and set back 10 feet from the actors. Since they were in close proximity to each other, the flooded Fresnel would backlight both.

Figure 12.15: *The HMI indoors.*

Remember our last exercise? Once you have your three-point lighting set, it is time to tweak the illumination and add additional lights. Both actors were wearing dark-blue pants and the filtered sunlight did little to bring that dark level up. We needed a light from the same direction as the sunlight to be pointed at their pants. Another 650-watt Arri Fresnel, not gelled blue, was pointed at the clothing. The orange cast of this tungsten light would not pose a problem on their blue pants.

Exercise Three

In this instance, you are to illuminate this scenario using the same lighting instrument we used—placed in a different arrangement. Try to create the sun streaming through the window on a cloudy day and accentuate the same look on a sunny day. The lighting instruments at your disposal are: one 2500-watt HMI, one 2K Fresnel, one 1K Fresnel in a Chimera-like enclosure, and two 650-watt Fresnels.

Exercise Four

Use the same scenario as before, but use different lighting instruments to make this a reality. Hint: Using more powerful lights is also an option (i.e., a 5000-watt HMI, 2K Chimera, etc).

Figure 12.16: *A disguised Arri.*

Even More Complicated

Still playing around with the lighting-the-same-fast-food-restaurant theme, this time we will have more actors involved and more obstacles to overcome. Just like in a real movie, we have to light for the master shot, close-ups, and the reversals.

Now we have three employees behind their cash registers at the fast food restaurant. The menu board is to be illuminated, but some of the panels do not have signs covering the fluorescent fixtures (I will give you some tricks to accomplish this feat). There will also be people in line behind the employees waiting to place their order.

When you shoot the reversal from the employees' point of view, as in most restaurants, the wall is lined with windows. To make the scenario slightly more difficult, you will be shooting this scene in March, where one day there is snow on the ground and the next day it is 70° and it all has melted.

The scene occurs during the day and there is a lot of activity in the restaurant. Hollywood often uses the same approach to lighting a scene like this, which is often explained in *American Cinematographer magazine*. Since there is so much daylight, it would be too time consuming to gel the windows and try to make this a tungsten production.

With a 2500-watt HMI used as a key source, it was raised to a height of 4 feet, gelled with ND6, and pointed at a 4 × 8-foot sheet of poster board. Foam core could also have been used, but at that size, poster board is much more manageable. Essentially, we now have a giant, soft bounce source that will still act as our key. This setup is out of frame, so it will still be the key for both master shots and close-ups (see Figure 12.17).

An HMI is one of the most versatile lighting instruments made; it has the ability to function in a multitude of settings. This light works as the key for the customers as well as the employees behind the counter. Using the same 1K Arri Fresnel in a Chimera-like enclosure, our off-camera fill light was gelled with booster blue to add a little warmth to the shot.

The same light could serve as the backlight for all three employees behind the counter. An Arri 650-watt Fresnel gelled with booster blue was elevated to a height of 8 feet and 15 feet from the employee closest to the camera, 11 feet from the middle person, and 5 feet from the woman closest to this light. Barn doors are necessary when trying to keep light where you do not want it. By marking the exact positions of the employees and angling the light carefully, we had our back/hair/shoulder light (see Figure 12.18).

Since we shot from the perspective of the customers first (for no particular reason), we will deal with tweaking the lighting behind the employees. A light was desperately needed to illuminate the area in the back where the cooks normally dwell. Leaving the overhead fluorescent fixtures illuminated was not strong enough to cast light from the bowels of the kitchen, and the eerie green cast of those lights would not add to the friendly atmosphere of our restaurant.

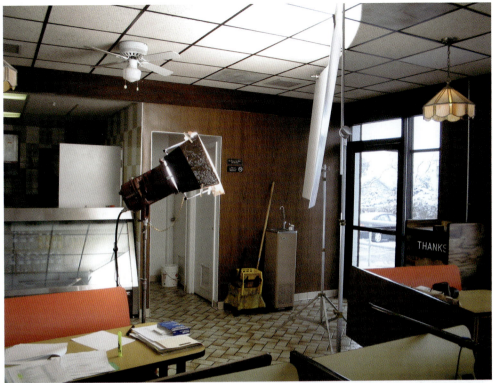

Figure 12.17: *An HMI used as a bounce light.*

Figure 12.18: *The backlight for the employees.*

Figure 12.19: *An Arri Fresnel erected in the back room.*

An Arri 650-watt Fresnel gelled with booster blue was placed far in the back by the deep fryers to simulate our light source, as seen in Figure 12.19. Raised to a height of 8 feet and placed 20 feet from the opening viewed by the restaurant patrons, we just wanted to show a slit of light as if there were life and activity in the back. Because we positioned the light so it was pointed at the fluorescent ceiling fixture, the viewer believes this is the light being cast from that practical. The illumination cast may be viewed in Figure 12.20. It actually looks like this is coming from the fluorescent.

Next, the menu display needed a lot of attention. Since the restaurant had been closed for months, most of the menu's lettering had vanished. All old, flickering fluorescent tubes were removed and replaced with new ones. Menus that were not visible had their lighting guts cannibalized to get the needed light tubes—that left us with vacant panels that looked horrible. You have two solutions to correct this: you can have new signs created to fill the void, or you can mask their appearance. We decided to use both options.

A local sign shop created a generic menu that really would not be visible from the camera's point of view. In close-ups, our depth of field would be too narrow for even those with the sharpest eyes to read them. The blank panels, without lights, were covered with 85ND6 gel cut to size. Straight ND6 gel is not dark enough, and the orange cast of the 85 was perfect to fill our blank

Figure 12.20: *The light from those dwelling in the back.*

spaces. The finished result, plus a few shines we corrected, may be seen in Figures 12.21 and 12.22.

Figure 12.23 shows another angle of our lighting setup as seen from the customer's point of view.

We were now about to tackle all of the camera angles from the customer's perspective. It is best to settle on one f-stop and light until that is what you achieve. In this case, my choice was f-5.6 and we lit until that is what we got. At times for the employee close-ups, I would put a 2 × 4-foot piece of foam core on a C-stand arm to add a little fill to the employee's face. Other than putting bounce cads on the counter or just out of frame, we had what we desired.

The reverse angle proved to be more challenging. Still using the 2500-watt HMI against the white board as our key, and the Chimera-like unit as our fill, we needed a little more light on the customer's faces. The backlight used for the employee's hair light (the Arri 650) was turned more to skim the faces of the customers. We were also getting ambient daylight through the side windows of the restaurant, but that fell off too quickly to be of much use. Instead, using new technology, I attached a 140-lamp LED Litepanel to the hot shoe of the camera (see Figure 12.24).

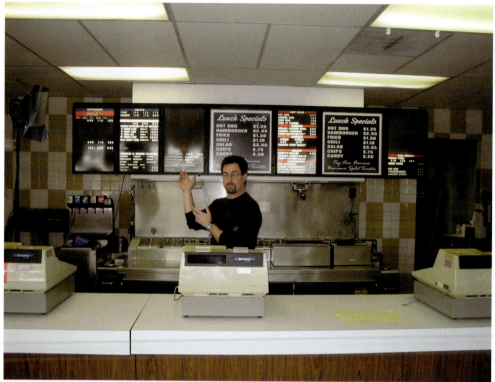

Figure 12.21: *Pat French proudly displays the improved signage.*

Figure 12.22: *Some customers on the scene.*

Figure 12.23: *Another angle of the lighting setup.*

Figure 12.24: *The Arri fill light and camera-mounted LED Litepanel.*

Figure 12.25: *85ND6 in an SUV's window.*

As mentioned in an earlier chapter, the LED light could be articulated to the correct position and dimmed as needed. The daylight balance added a twinkle in the customer's eyes that only a small light at close proximity can do.

The biggest problem now was not so much the intense daylight viewed through the rear windows, but dealing with what was happening outdoors. Through the glass, the illumination outside was f-11, still only 2 stops above our interior. But the "view" needed to be changed.

Not having shades, we needed to block the cars on the street as well as the restaurant's sign. By parking the soundman's SUV on the sidewalk, we blocked most of what we saw out of one window. From the camera's point of view, it did not look like the SUV was parked on the side-walk. However, the light coming through his driver-side window still gave away our secret. Tom again solved the problem by cutting a piece of 85ND6 and attaching it to the driver's window to cut the light (see Figure 12.25). We did the same thing to a car parked across the street. By putting a piece of 85ND6 under the windshield's wipers, the glint of the chrome and glass was removed.

Pieces of foam core placed in the window acted as pretend "signs" to partially block the view (the backs of most signs are white anyway), and all that remained was the snow or lack thereof.

This scene was shot over the course of a few days, and the snow came and went even though consistency was necessary. If snow was visible and needed to be removed, we used brooms to knock all of the white stuff off the bushes, shrubs, and cars.

If we needed snow to match another shot and there was none around, we used large pieces of foam core on the grass as snow, or bundled cotton draped over trees and shrubs. From a distance it was impossible to distinguish this from the real thing.

An ever-mindful eye is needed in the viewfinder to watch for these and other distractions.

Exercise Five

Using the same lighting instruments—one 2500-watt HMI, one 4 × 8-foot piece of foam core, one 1K Fresnel in a Chimera-like box, two 650-watt Fresnels, and an LED Litepanel—create the same look for both angles.

Exercise Six

This should be easy! Now light everyone using different instruments and keep them from baking under the lights.

Under the Colored Lights

There will be times when colored gels are necessary to make a shoot come alive. Our next scenario deals with an exercise video, where brightly colored lights are the norm.

Our space was on a stage, but the same lighting could apply to any interior location. Several talented instructors will be going through their routine, and eventually the viewer will be watching this all on his or her home TV. The background/backdrop should be nondescript and blend into the environment. The lighting must be high-key and happy, much like a sitcom.

Our background was no more than an off-white curtain, but you could use a muslin backdrop just as easily. With three 1500-watt MoleFar Super Quartz Cyc strips, each connected to a light board, we chose to illuminate the white background curtain first. With rose-colored gel in each, we bathed the curtain in a vibrant rose hue. With each dimmer set at 50%, we did not want the set to look like the Red Light District.

Four prop columns were placed against the curtain with a 200-watt inky behind each, gelled orange, and pointed upward. Attached to a pigeon, each light would stay hidden behind the column.

Doing things in reverse, we set the backlight first. A 350-watt Arri Fresnel extended to 9 feet was pointed at the talent 11 feet away. With 216 diffusion on the Fresnel, the talent's blonde hair radiated. The fill was also an Arri Fresnel, this time a 650-watt unit 9 feet up and 8 feet from the talent. A ½ scrim was used to cut the light's output.

Her key was a 1K Fresnel in the soft fabric of a Chimera. Although high-key, the illumination still had to be flattering. Only 4 feet from the talent and raised to a height of 6 feet, we now had an f-8 exposure (see Figure 12.29). See Figure 12.26 to see our finished shot.

Another variation on this same scenario is lighting a group of instructors, using a mixture of grid and kit lighting. Figure 12.27 shows our set before we began lighting. Note the black Duvetyn screens to hide the rest of the set.

In Figure 12.28, we added the colored lights, activated the Jumbo Trons (large video display monitors). Now it began looking more like a real set. With all six of the instructors on the set, each needed to have their own backlight. Therefore six 1000-watt Molequartz Molelipso lights were brought into action. Depending on the instructor's hair color, the individual units were dimmed until we were happy. The same key and fill from the single shot were incorporated—just moved back slightly (see Figure 12.30).

When the instructor grouping was reduced to four, we now used four backlights and the same key and fill. It is easy to make variations to your setup if using a lighting board and multiple units (see Figure 12.31).

Sometimes just changing the background gel color (to blue in this case) can give your set a whole different look. If your lights have automated gel rings, a push of a button gives you a different hue (see Figure 12.32).

Exercise Seven

Using the same units—one Chimera with a 1K, one 650-watt Fresnel, one 350-watt Fresnel, four inkys, six 1000-watt Molelipsos (Leko), and three 1500-watt Quartz Cyc strips—change the lighting from my initial setup. Hint: This was our only tungsten setup—it does not have to be that way.

Exercise Eight

Now find your own units (not what I used) and make this set sing!

Up Close and Personal

This last scenario is an example of lighting an intimate interview without blinding the talent. This is much like the technique used in *Dateline* and *20/20* for their setups. The lighting should be soft and bounced. Any age, sex, or skin tone works well with this type of lighting.

Figure 12.26: *Colored lights and exercise can make you healthy.*

Figure 12.27: *Our set before lighting.*

Figure 12.28: *See what a difference a color light makes.*

Figure 12.29: *Frank Baker and our key light.*

Figure 12.30: *Six instructors, six back lights.*

Figure 12.31: *Which two instructors are missing?*

Figure 12.32: *Changing the background color for a different look.*

Figure 12.33: *A soft, key light for interviews.*

The interviewer and interviewee usually sit facing each other with a camera dedicated to each person. Our key would be an Arri 650-watt Fresnel in a Chimera for each individual. Raised to a height of 6 feet and 5 feet from the seated talent, this would serve well (see Figure 12.33).

The fill was a Flexifill 24-inch diameter reflector (using the white rather than the gold side) clamped to a light stand. Each person would have their own fill. The closer to the person, the more fill light (ours was three feet away at eye level) (see Figure 12.34).

Our backlight for each was a 150-watt Dedolight with a hand-cut cookie made from Blackwrap. This created a mottled pattern on the subject's shoulders. Sometimes this extra texture is unseen, but perceived anyway (see Figure 12.35).

The end result is seen in Figure 12.36. With one of the talent missing, you get an idea what the lighting may look like.

Exercise Nine

Your version using the same lighting should include two 1K Chimeras, two Flexifills, and two 150-watt Dedolights.

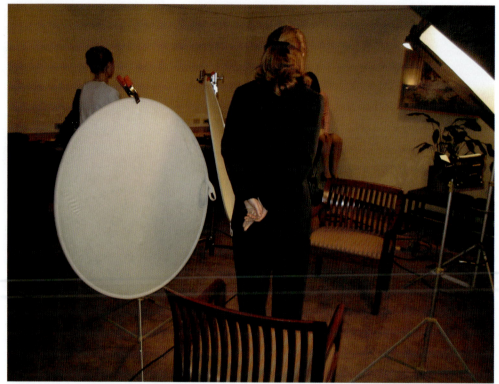

Figure 12.34: *Using Flexifill as a bounce.*

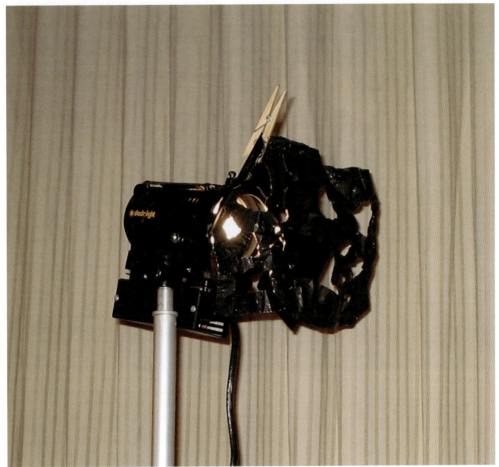

Figure 12.35: *Our Dedolight with Blackwrap cookie used as a backlight.*

Figure 12.36: *The actual setup for an interview.*

Exercise Ten

This lighting style is very popular and may be used on almost every project; it is a good idea to see if you can come up with several variations on how to light an interview.

Hopefully, this chapter was helpful in your quest to light some key scenarios. Chapter 13 will help hammer home some concepts with the Glossary.

Chapter 13
Glossary, Terms and Tips
Control Yourself

These goodies are used on location and in the studio to control spill (unwanted light), alter the quality of the light, or provide mounting support. Some are physically attached to the instrument and some are placed in front on a separate stand to alter or control its output. There are also a number of accessories that are helpful in mounting instruments under a variety of circumstances. There are also many widgets that are just plain helpful in getting the job done. My list is by no means complete, but represents basic and commonly used items.

Ace is not a hardware store. It is a 1000-watt Fresnel, also known as a "baby."

ANSI stands for American National Standards Institute. It is an independent association formed to promote consistency and interchangeability among manufacturers of lamps and lighting equipment. Though various manufacturers have different numbers for the same type of lamp, the manufacturer's number can be referenced to an ANSI number to determine if it is interchangeable with a lamp from another company.

Apple boxes are not designed for fruit storage. They are multipurpose wooden boxes that may be utilized for sitting and standing and for prop elevation. They are glued, nailed, and constructed with internal center supports so that they can withstand hefty loads. They come in a variety of graduated sizes. A full apple is 8 inches high, a half-apple is 4 inches high, and a quarter-apple is 2 inches high. They form convenient bases for low-angle lights and hi-hat camera mounts, or for leading men who can't quite measure up to the height of their leading ladies.

Asbestos gloves are made of a heavy, heat-resisting material and they will prevent many a burn. They may also cause cancer, so stay away from them. They are no longer sold.

Figure 13.1: *Baby combo.*

Lighting instruments are potentially dangerous if handled improperly or placed too close to other objects. They are very hot. A 750-watt tungsten halogen filament burns at a temperature of 5300°F. The outside wall temperature of a lamp is 1100°F. The temperature of accessories placed in the gate of a Leko is 1575°F. You need protection when working with these temperatures. Thin cloth gloves won't do! Buy heavy-duty work gloves or gloves with leather fingers and thumbs.

Baby is a 1000-watt Fresnel, also known as an "ace" (see Figure 13.1).

Barn doors are black metal flaps attached to an instrument or placed in the accessory shoe on the front of it. They are used to restrict the coverage area of a light source. There are usually two or four flaps that can shape the lighted area. Sometimes they are permanently attached to the instrument, as with some portable broads, or they may attach to the front of an instrument in a bracket provided for that purpose. The best units are able to turn 360° around the opening of the fixture to provide more flexible-pattern positioning. They produce a diffused cut-off line. They absorb much heat, so use your gloves when you try to adjust them (see Figure 13.2).

Figure 13.2: *Barn doors on a Lowel Omni.*

Base light is a diffuse light level on a set that permits the camera to operate efficiently, without producing noise in the dark areas.

Batten is a horizontal pipe from which lighting instruments or scenery are hung.

Bazooka is not a gun or bubble gum. It is a method of supporting lighting instruments over the edge of the catwalk in a sound stage. It looks like an extension arm for a C–stand, and it fits into holes that are predrilled in the catwalk.

Best boy may in fact be a girl or an old codger. He or she is a crew member whose duties include repair of broken connectors, switches, or cables. He or she replaces bulbs in lights and lamps in less beefy instruments, and cleans and adjusts instruments to make sure they are ready when needed.

Blackbody is the theoretical standard used to determine the color temperature of incandescent light sources (see "Color Temperature" in Chapter 1).

Blackwrap is a heavy-duty matte black aluminum foil packaged in a tear-off roll just as household aluminum wrap is. It is used to wrap around areas of a lighting instrument that are projecting spill on some area of the set or is used as a flag, a cutter, or emergency barn doors. It's better than regular aluminum foil because it withstands the high temperatures of lighting instruments, and its matte black finish does not produce objectionable reflections anywhere around the set (however, it sometimes smokes when it is first used). It is available from Great American Market and Rosco (see the Appendix) (see Figures 13.3 and 13.4).

Borderlight is also called an "X-ray." It is a striplight that is mounted above the acting area. Primarily used in theater, these same instruments may be used on the floor in front of the acting area as footlights or on the floor upstage as cyc lights.

Bounce cards are matte white reflectors used to redirect the light onto the subject after it has left the source. They can also be used to redirect wasted spill to an area where it is required, without the need for an additional instrument. Any reasonably stiff material will do. Foam board or Foam core is lightweight, easy to cut, and will stay put when placed in a gobo head and carefully positioned. Since the bounce light from a card is so diffuse, these cards must be placed close to the area you wish to light, just outside camera frame.

Bull switch is a master circuit breaker or fuse box with manual disconnect switch used at the head end of an electrical tie-in system. It is placed between the entrance panel from which the power is taken and your distribution system to provide protection and permit complete power-down of all your equipment.

Butterflys or "overheads" are large rectangular aluminum frames over which you can stretch a variety of materials to diffuse sunlight or natural light on exterior or interior locations. They may be as large as 20 feet on a side, and cover an area large enough to permit shooting close-ups or medium shots. They work well in studios when placed between multiple instruments and a subject, such as a car. They eliminate multiple-source reflections from the shiny compound curved surface (see Figure 13.8).

Cameo or "limbo lighting" is a style in which only the foreground area is lit. The background is allowed to go black (as seen in Figures 6.1 through 6.4). It is a dramatic form that is economical because of the lack of scenery, and it keeps the viewer focused on the people or products without any distracting elements.

Chasers are lamps that are placed in a multicircuit string and connected to a control device that turns every fourth or fifth lamp on and off in sequence, to create the illusion that the lamps are moving in a forward or backward direction. Such arrangements are commonly used around marquees, signs, or runways to draw attention.

C-clamps derive their name from their shape, and they are used when extremely secure quick mounting is required. Nothing works as well. They come in 4-inch, 6-inch, and 8-inch sizes. True lighting C-clamps have one or more ⅝-inch studs welded to their frame to facilitate the attachment of portable lighting instruments.

Figure 13.3: *Blackwrap.*

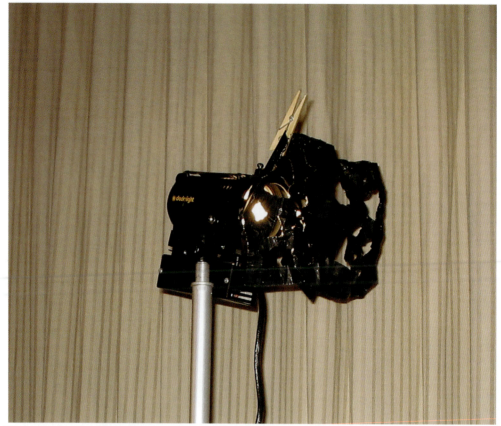

Figure 13.4: *Blackwrap used as a cookie.*

C-Stand is short for "Century Stand." It has three legs (each one slightly higher and longer than the next) that can be folded flat in a 90° angle to the shaft and nested to make transport easier. These legs are spring-loaded and snap into their working position quickly for setup. The shortest leg can be set under most furniture and the tallest leg can fit over or around various other stands or items on set. Though they are somewhat expensive, they are extremely sturdy, take a real beating, and are well worth the cost. Available in several different sizes, they are a must on every set.

Cliplock is an alligator-type connector used to attach the leads for your electrical tie-in system to the bus bars of the entrance panel. These special connectors provide a very strong mechanical connection that cannot be pulled off their point of attachment. A bolt arrangement ensures that the clip will not open.

Color frames or gel frames are thin, rectangular sheet-metal sandwiches that have a large hole in the middle. They are used to hold color filters such as gel, diffusion material, heat filters, or neutral density or color-correction media. In most cases, they slide into the bracket that is used to attach barn doors. Both barn doors and color frames can be used at the same time, if desired. In some of the more portable fixtures, such as the Lowel lights, they are collapsi-

Figure 13.5: *Color frame.*

ble frames with clips to hold the filter and diffusion materials mentioned. They prevent instrument heat from warping the material immediately and destroying it (see Figure 13.5).

Cookie (pronounced KOOK'-ee) or "cucoloris" (pronounced kook-a-LOR'-is) is used to create a shadow pattern on backdrops and/or subjects. Positioned in front of a light source, it breaks up an evenly or flatly lit area into interesting pools of light and shadow. You can buy commercially produced cookies made of ¼-inch plywood painted black or you can fashion your own out of tagboard or Foam core using a utility knife. Be careful not to place such homemade units too close to the light source as they may scorch. Greater separation also permits a sharper focus of the projected pattern (see Figure 13.6).

Cyc light is a special, high-intensity form of flood or broad that is used to illuminate cycloramas (see Chapter 10 and Figure 13.7).

Cyclorama or cyc is a cloth or plaster surface that is used to surround the acting area and to create the illusion of infinite depth (see Chapter 10).

Deuce is one up on an ace. It is a 2000-watt Fresnel; also known as a "junior."

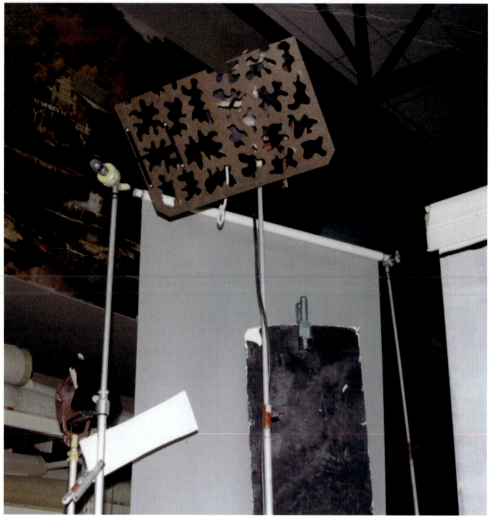

Figure 13.6: *Cucoloris.*

Figure 13.7: *Cyc lights strip with stage paddles (Photo courtesy of Mole-Richardson Co.).*

Figure 13.8: *A butterfly over food.*

Diffusion material is used to produce diffuse light. Made from a variety of substances, it will alter the quality of light that passes through it, making it more diffuse, producing less dense shadows, and creating light that falls off more rapidly. It can be purchased in precut squares or as roll material. You can place it in a color frame or suspend it in front of an instrument using various other devices.

Dimmers are used to lower the voltage applied to the filament of a lamp and lessen its intensity. While they are mandatory for creating a variety of effects, they also reduce the lamp's rated color temperature and are not an acceptable method of reducing intensity of talent light (see Figure 13.9).

Dinky is a 200-watt, 3-inch Fresnel with a sheet metal frame (see the discussion of Inky).

Dots are small round wire loops attached to a wire handle, something like the device children use for blowing bubbles. They can be covered with a variety of things, from thin netting or wire scrim to opaque material, and are used to control or eliminate a specular highlight and other lighting problems. Like flags, they are held between the source and the subject by gobo heads. Unlike flags, their small size affects only a limited portion of the lighted area. They are usually available in 3-inch, 6-inch, and 10-inch diameter sizes (see Figure 13.10).

Downstage is the area of the stage that is nearest the audience. The term stems from the early Greek theater where the stage was actually racked. The stage floor nearest the audience was

Figure 13.9: *Dimmer (Photo courtesy of Lowel-Light Manufacturing, Inc.).*

Figure 13.10: *Dots (Photo courtesy of Mole-Richardson Co.).*

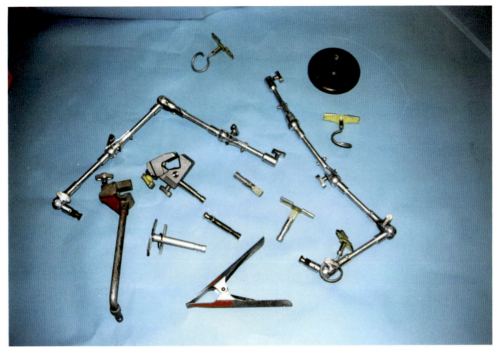

Figure 13.11: *Drop ceiling scissor clamp and cable holder.*

lower than the floor farther from it. In this way, as actors walked away from the audience, they were not hidden behind foreground players.

Dressing cables is a phrase used to describe the act of arranging the path of lighting and sound cables so that they do not interfere with traffic patterns on the set or appear in the shot. It is important to dress and tape cables out of harm's way, especially if you have to run them down halls and across doorways in an office building or other public area. It is not advisable to dress audio and lighting cables alongside each other. That frequently introduces a 60-cycle hum in the audio. In effect, what you do when you place these cables parallel to one another over any distance is create a giant transformer. Place either cable over the top of the other to create a cross; this will eliminate the hum. Gaffer tape should be used to dress cables where foot traffic might cause a problem.

Drop ceiling scissor clamp and cable holder is a mount designed to close with a scissor action over conventional T-bar drop ceiling frames. It is fitted with a standard ⅝-inch stud to allow mounting of lightweight location fixtures. Some studs also contain brackets that can be used to drape electrical cords across the ceiling without the need for tape or other unreliable antigravity devices—a necessary device in every grip kit (see Figure 13.11).

Edison plug or "Edison outlet" is the term given to the traditional grounded plugs or wall outlets used in the home (U.S. and Canada). The outlets contain two parallel slots of different lengths. The longer of the two outlet slots or the wider of the two plug prongs correspond to the neutral wire of the circuit. The outlets have a circular ground hole that mates with the ground pin of the plug. Outlets with one T-shaped slot indicate a 20-amp

Figure 13.12: *Ellipsoidal (Photo courtesy of Mole-Richardson Co.).*

capacity circuit. These outlets do not require a special plug to mate with this T-slot. Efforts to defeat the grounding and polarity aspects of such plugs and outlets are not a good idea. The polarized aspect of the prongs and the grounding pin can prevent nasty shocks in the event of cable or equipment failure.

Egg crates are not used for storage of poultry products. They are deep, wooden frames that form several cubicles, and they are placed in front of a softlight to diffuse the light rays even further.

Electrician is the crew member responsible for bringing the power from its source to the lighting instruments through the distribution system. The source may be a tie-in, a temporary drop, or a generator.

Ellipsoidal or "Leko" is a lighting instrument with an elliptical reflector and a complex lens system that makes it possible to place light exactly where you want it without the need for any external accessories to control spill. A series of shutters, an iris, or a gobo can be sharply focused onto an area of the set (see Figure 13.12).

Fill light is the diffuse light placed to reduce the contrast of the shadows cast by the key light. It should never be bright enough to cast its own shadow. If for some reason it does cast a shadow, the instrument should be placed so that the resulting shadow falls out of range of the camera.

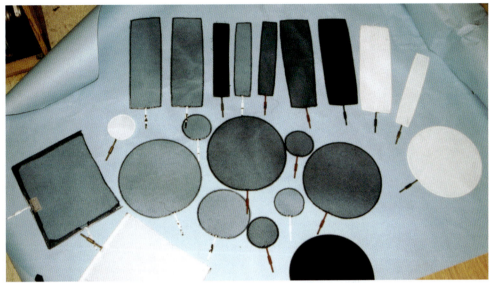

Figure 13.13: *Fingers and dots.*

Fingers are similar to dots in function, but they are long, thin rectangles of material used to block light on a rectangular portion of the subject. They come in 2 × 12-inch and 4 × 14-inch sizes. They are covered with a variety of diffusion materials (see Figure 13.13).

Flags or "cutters" are square frames covered with opaque material to block light from certain areas. Such unwanted light is called "spill." Flags are placed in front of an instrument on a stand of their own and positioned to cut the light where needed. Depending on their placement, they offer a more defined cut-off point than barn doors because they can be positioned farther away from the front of the instrument. Cutters are similar to flags except that they are like large fingers, long and narrow.

French flag is a term given to flags that are made of metal rather than opaque material or some form of scrim material. They are the type of flags provided in the Lowel kits (see Figure 13.14).

Frezzi is a well-known and well-respected battery-operated, camera-mounted light. Frezzolini was the first firm to produce a rugged camera-mounted DC light for news coverage and the name is often used in a generic sense to describe any such instrument regardless of the manufacturer (see Figure 13.15).

Gaffer is not the person responsible for making mistakes. He is responsible for designing a lighting plot for each scene after consulting with the director, the director of photography, or the camera operator. After the plot is approved, the gaffer directs the laying of cables and puts the instruments that are going to be used in place at the proper height. At that point, the grips take over.

Gaffer grips are like large, metal, spring-operated clothespins. They have one or more standard ⅜-inch studs attached to them and are designed to hold lightweight instruments or accessories in position on pipes, the edge of doors and other objects around the set (see Figure 13.16).

Figure 13.14: *French flag.*

Gaffer tape is a specially formulated 2-inch wide cloth tape, available in several colors, and commonly confused with duct tape or furnace tape found at the local hardware store. Duct tape is not the same and should not be substituted. Gaffer tape will not damage painted or stained wood surfaces, and will not leave a sticky residue. It can be used for anything from securing cables to mending the leading lady's dress. It can be applied to silver subjects such as car bumpers to reduce glare, and it looks convincing on camera. Duct tape is too shiny for this purpose. Always have plenty of gaffer tape on hand.

Gobo can mean different things, depending on who is speaking. Lighting directors are probably talking about a precut metal disk that is inserted in the gate of a special pattern projector or Leko to project a specific image on the set or actors. These come in a wide

Figure 13.15: *Frezzi (Photo courtesy of Lowel-Light Manufacturing, Inc.).*

assortment of effects, ranging from fireworks displays and American flags to venetian blinds and trees (see the Appendix).

Grips talking about gobos are probably referring to a Tinker-toy-like metal disk that is fastened to the extension arm of an accessory stand. Gobo heads or grip heads are available in 2½-inch or 4½-inch diameters. They mount on standard ⅝-inch pins and are designed to receive ⅝-inch, ½-inch, and ⅜-inch round accessories. They will also accept irregular shapes and flat objects like handmade flags of Foam core.

Just for fun, if camera operators are talking, they would be referring to some object in the foreground of the set that the camera will shoot through, or move past while shooting the scene. It may be a decorative screen or the andirons of a fireplace.

Audio technicians are probably referring to portable sound deadening panels that can be placed around individual musicians in a studio to isolate the sound of their instrument

Photometrics or performance data are light output specifications for a lighting instrument. They state the intensity of the light produced at various distances from the source and indicate the area covered at the stated distances. If the instrument is a focusing spot, that information will be given for the full spot position, the full flood position, and possibly for a midrange setting. This information may be presented in a simple numeric chart, with graphic drawings or with photos of the coverage area in addition to printed statistics.

Pigeon is a small metal plate with a 2⅝-inch rod extending upward. This unit acts as a light stand. Perfect for Inkys, a pigeon lets you place a light extremely close to the floor.

Practical is a term used to describe any lighting fixture or prop on stage that actually works. Items such as table lamps or radios can be practical.

Reflector boards are designed to redirect natural or artificial light. They generally have two sides or faces that offer specular and diffuse reflective, in either silver or gold surfaces. The silver side produces a harsher, colder (blue) reflection, whereas the gold side produces a softer, warmer (orange) look. They are like bounce cards, but their output is more specular, and they have greater throw. They are normally covered with smooth silver foil on the "hard" side and textured silver leaf on the "soft" side. Gold leaf is also available. The warm tone of its reflection is very complimentary to dark skin.

Sand bags provide additional weight to C-stand bases and other portable objects that could easily fall over if not weighted down. They are traditionally filled with sand and weigh between 15 and 35 pounds. If a sand bag leaks during a shipment with cameras and recorders, it can wreak havoc with the technical gear. For this reason, it is best to use shot bags that contain small, metal BBs instead. If you extend your stands, use shot bags.

Scrims or "nets" are nonelectrical dimmers. They provide a controllable means of reducing light output without affecting color temperature or generating radio frequency interference. Open-end scrim frames are made of spring steel to provide constant tension on the exposed cloth edge. The open end facilitates feathering or blending the edge of the light beam without causing a harsh line. A lavender scrim causes a 15% light reduction. Singles reduce light output by about 30%. Doubles cut back by about 50%. Exact effect depends on placement. Some are made of cloth mesh, others are made of silk. They can be held in front of the source by gobo or grip heads on C-stands.

Sliding rod is an economical means of adjusting the height of lighting instruments hung from a grid. The rods come in different lengths that allow you to raise or lower the instrument by releasing a thumb screw on a sliding ring that is fastened to the fixture. Lights hung from a pantograph can be adjusted from the floor by using a stick. Lights fastened to a sliding rod must be adjusted from a ladder and require a great deal of time to set up. Unlike the pantograph, which collapses as the light is raised, the sliding rod remains the same length regardless of how high the instrument is placed, and it may hang down in front of some other light and cast a shadow on the set. Some sliding rods telescope into shorter lengths (see Figure 13.18).

Snoots are cylindrically shaped attachments resembling stovepipes. They are attached to the front of the instrument in the color frame bracket. They confine and narrow the light produced by a spot or flood (see Figure 13.19).

Figure 13.18: *Sliding rod with head grip.*

Spike is not something you do to a volleyball, and it's not the network for men. It is the act of placing a piece of tape on the floor to indicate where some prop or piece of furniture should be placed, or to indicate where an actor should stand so he will be in the right position for lighting and camera shots. The actor's spike mark is usually two pieces of tape in the shape of a "T." When he hits the mark, he places one foot on either side of the leg of the T, facing in the direction of the T's crosspiece.

Spill is a term for light that falls on some area of the set where it is not wanted. Somewhat like a child's milk.

Stage box is a rectangular-shaped porcelain receptacle in a heavy metal box used to distribute moderately heavy loads of current. It comes in a variety of capacities and configurations. Stage plugs or paddles are inserted into the stage box to tap a portion of the available current.

Stage left is an instruction describing movement or a location to the left of actors as they face the audience or the camera. Stage right shouldn't need any explanation.

Stage plugs are heavy-duty insulated plugs used with stage boxes for the distribution of current around the set. Large brass strips on each side of these plugs make contact with the brass

Figure 13.19: *Snoot.*

lining of the stage box. Generally, the stage plug is on one end of an extension and nineteen hundred boxes are connected to the other end for distribution through standard Edison outlets.

Sticks is slang for a "camera's tripod."

Strike means to remove something from the stage area and place it out of the way. It is also used to describe the action of packing up your equipment or taking down a set for storage or disposal.

Teners are not opera singers. They are 10,000-watt Fresnels (see Figure 13.20).

Tree is a high stand with horizontal arms and a very heavy metal base from which lighting instruments can be hung. Generally used in theaters, it can be employed on any location to mount one or more instruments from the same stand. Sometimes, small tower-like structures for mounting instruments are also referred to as trees.

Trick Y is a Y-shaped cable arrangement used to split a single leg of an electrical distribution system into two legs.

Figure 13.20: *Tener (Photo courtesy of Mole-Richardson Co.).*

Umbrellas are made of a textured silver fabric like that used in portable softlight reflectors. They make it possible to use spotlights and broads as sources for diffuse light. You simply aim the fixtures at the inside of the umbrella when it is open. The reflected output is very soft and uncontrollable. Like any diffuse light, it falls off quickly so you must be able to position it near your subject. Open-faced instruments work best as sources for umbrellas. If you are using a focusing spot, do not put it in the full spot setting as it may destroy the umbrella material due to excessive heat. Fresnels can be used as sources for umbrellas by removing the lens (see Figure 13.23).

Upstage is the area of the stage that is farthest from the audience (see "downstage"). When used as a verb, it means that one actor is pulling focus or audience attention away from another at a time when this actor should not have the attention.

Work lights are permanently installed general lighting fixtures in a studio or stage and are used to provide light for setups and general work on set. They should always be turned off during shooting since they are not color-corrected and will cast multiple shadows and unwanted spill.

Zip is not a postal code. It is a 2000-watt (or less) portable softlight or a name applied to a common household lamp cord, called "zip cord" (see Figure 13.21).

See Figure 13.22 for an example of a completed lighting setup.

Figure 13.21: *Zip (Photo courtesy of Lowel-Light Manufacturing, Inc.).*

Your Gadget Bag

In many cases, location lighting is an unplanned event. You are told to "go to Widgets, Inc. in East Nowhere and shoot Mr. Bumfutz and his two assistants as they take a Widget from the drawing board to the shipping clerk." With little advance information, you are driven to the airport with 22 cases of assorted goodies hoping you have what you need. You might, or you might not. If you don't, improvise. That's the excitement and satisfaction of the job. Lest you become too excited or satisfied, a few things can save you anxious moments.

Carry your own gadget bag and keep it filled with those little things that make the unexpected manageable. I use the term "bag" loosely because I've found that keeping these items in a canvas bag defeats the idea of being organized. If everything is thrown into a bag it makes it difficult to find the specific item you need. You are also likely to leave something behind when

Figure 13.22: *Equipment on the set.*

Figure 13.23: *Umbrellas on the set.*

you strike everything and pack up to go home. You can't tell from looking into a bag if everything is there.

From a canvas bag I progressed to a metal box with various compartments so things could be organized and I could tell at a glance if something was missing. That created a problem at airports. I now carry a small compartmentalized briefcase that can be X-rayed and placed under an airline seat or in the overhead compartment. If I am driving to a shoot, I still use the metal case.

Here are some suggested items that can make your life easier. They are not presented in any particular order of importance. In fact, the most important item is the one you don't have.

1. Take along a number of triplets or "3fers," also called "cube taps," which allow you to plug three things into a single outlet or extension cord. Buy the heavy-duty, grounded type (gray, blue, or orange). The lower the gauge, the better.
2. Keep a good number of adapters with you that will allow you to plug grounded equipment into ungrounded outlets. Never break off ground pins to accomplish this mismatch. It's unsafe and unprofessional!
3. Keep an analog or digital Volt-Ohm meter to check voltage, fuses, lamps, and cords for continuity. Take along a spare battery for your meter. Just when you need the meter most, the battery will die and you will be in Littletown, USA on a Sunday with all the stores closed.
4. A helpful item to have is a plug-in, three-wire outlet analyzer. It looks like a grounded male plug with three indicator lights to show the condition of an outlet without probes or meters. You can confirm working circuits and check for wiring faults like open ground or hot wires and reversed polarity.
5. Be sure to carry some tools. An adjustable wrench and a small screwdriver set with Phillips and regular blades will be invaluable in making last-minute repairs. A set of Allen wrenches is also a good investment. Often, the focus knobs of instruments are secured or semi-secured by Allen screws. Leatherman or some less expensive imitators allow you to carry almost every tool in a pouch attached to your belt.
6. Have plenty of spring-clamped clothespins to hold filters, gels, or diffusion material to the front of lighting instruments or barn doors. Be sure to use the wooden version. The newer plastic type will melt down almost immediately and produce a foul smell on the set. Burning wooden clothespins smell better. When using any type of clothespin (wooden or plastic), make sure they are not attached too close to the light source. The farther you attach the clothespins from the source of heat, the less chance of burning.
7. Take black, white, or yellow china markers along. They allow you to write on metal and glass surfaces and mark reference points on the video monitor, the waveform monitor, or the vectorscope. You can mark focus and zoom stops on the lens barrel and use them for a variety of other tasks.
8. A small roll of white surgical tape. This tape can be ripped into small pieces and attached to the lens to mark focal positions and possibly help an errant doctor.

9. Don't forget the can of dulling spray. If you do, there's sure to be a stainless steel tank in the background of three shots. Something that works even better to cut down glare on bright metal surfaces is hair spray. Hair spray in aerosol cans is available at many drug stores.

10. You will always find use for a roll of clothesline rope and some heavy twine.

11. Monofilament fishing line will allow you to suspend things invisibly and trigger certain special effects from off camera.

12. Rubber doorstops have many uses. They can keep doors open, such as doors that lock when closed and doors that can't be opened without a special key that is not around. They can level props for the camera and keep things from moving off their marks.

13. A utility knife can cut cheese and pizzas to make life during breaks more livable. It also comes in handy for cutting color media and filter material, as well as for stripping wires and cutting ropes, tape, and Foam core. You can also use it to carve out a gobo.

14. To keep cords and ropes neat, there is nothing better than a large supply of Lowel-Clips, those plastic wonders that don't leave a sticky mess on your cables.

15. Several rolls of gaffer tape are a must. It comes in yellow, blue, green, silver, black, white, and several fluorescent colors. Have plenty on hand to tape and mask a variety of things on set.

16. Double-stick foam tape is a good thing to keep throw rugs from living up to their name. It can also fasten lightweight pictures to walls and keep frames from tilting. Almost anything that slips out of place can be tamed using this product.

17. Always carry spare video connectors like RCA to BNC, BNC to RCA, splitters, barrels, and any other type of video or audio connector you may need. Ten minutes in a Radio Shack before the shoot will keep you from losing your hair on the set. Also carry spare BNC and audio cables. They are easily misplaced and very embarrassing if you forget them.

18. It is a good idea to carry small squares of different types of diffusion materials, 85, ND in various stops, and some booster blue to gel individual instruments or treat small window areas or practical instruments on set.

19. Although not a lighting item, carry a spare set of ear buds (earphones). These are not extremely comfortable, but they come in handy for checking audio levels in a pinch and can make you new sound people friends on a shoot.

More items will appear in the bag as you find you need them on a shoot.

Beyond Your Gadget Bag

There are some larger items that won't fit in your bag, but they should travel with you as excess baggage if you are flying.

1. Always have plenty of spare lamps in a variety of wattages. They permit you to use the lowest wattage lamp necessary for a given location to keep heat and current consumption as low as possible.

2. Take plenty of extension cords. Put them on simple reels. If the budget permits, it is best to have retractable cord reels to save time in setup and strike. The best kinds to use are those that have a fan-shaped 3-outlet head to permit several fixtures to be connected to a single-source outlet.

3. If you will be shooting on a location involving windows or glass doors, carry rolls of 85 gel to convert daylight to 3200°K. You should also have a roll of ND filter material in several densities and a roll of booster blue to convert 3200°K lamps to daylight. They should be in individual shipping tubes to protect them from scratches and kinking.

Appendix

Resources for the Lighting Professional

The firms listed in this section represent a cross-section of companies that manufacture, rent or sell products that are used by lighting professionals. Some may have branch offices nearer to you than those listed. You will find them very helpful when you need solutions to the various lighting problems you encounter. Don't hesitate to give them a call to discuss a product you want more information about, or to seek advice for a specific problem. *The addresses, websites, and phone numbers were accurate at the time of printing.*

Alan Gordon Enterprises
1430 Cahuenga Blvd.
Hollywood, CA 90028
213/466-3561
www.alangordon.com

Altman Stage Lighting Co.
57 Alexander St.
Yonkers, NY 10701
914/476-7987
www.altmanltg.com

Anton Bauer
1 Controls Dr.
Shelton, CT 06484
203/929-1100
www.antonbauer.com

Arriflex Corp.
500 Rte. 303
Blauvelt, NY 10913
914/353-1400
www.arri.com

Barbizon
426 W. 55th St.
New York, NY 10019
212/258-1620
www.barbizon.com

Bardwell & McAllister
7051 Santa Monica Blvd.
Hollywood, CA 90038
213/466-9361
No Website

Belden Communications, Inc.
534 W. 25th St.
New York, NY 10001
212/691-1910
www.belden.com

Bogen Photo Corp.
17-20 Willow St.
Fairlawn, NJ 07014
201/794-6500
www.bogenphoto.com

Cinema Products Corp.
2037 Granville Ave.
Los Angeles, CA 90023
213/478-0711
www.steadicam.com

Cinemills Corp.
3500 Magnolida Blvd.
Burbank, CA 91505
818/843-4560
www.cinemills.org

Cine 60
630 9th Ave.
New York, NY 10036
212/586-8782
www.cine601.visualnet.com

Colortran
1015 Chestnut St.
Burbank, CA 90506
818/843-1200
www.colortran.com

Comprehensive Video Supply
148 Veterans Dr.
Northvale, NJ 07647
201/767-7990
www.compvideo.com

Cool-Lux Lighting Industries
5723 Auckland Ave.
North Hollywood, CA 91601
818/761-6166
www.cool-lux.com

DeSisti Americas
328 Adams St.
Hoboken, NJ 07030
201/792-4980
www.desisti.it

Frezzolini Electronics
5/7 Valley St.
Hawthorne, NJ 07506
201/427-1106
www.frezzi.co

General Electric
Nela Park
Cleveland, OH 44112
216/266-2122
www.ge.com

Grand Stage Lighting Co.
630 W. Lake St.
Chicago, IL 60606
312/332-5611
www.grandstage.com

Imero Fiorentino Assoc.
6430 Sunset Blvd., No. 618
Los Angeles, CA 90028
213/467-4020
No Website

Imero Fiorentino Assoc.
44 W. 63rd St.
New York, NY 10023
212/246-0600
No Website

Kino Flo, Inc.
10848 Cantara Street
Sun Valley, CA 91352
818/767-6528
www.kinoflo.com

Lee America
534 W. 25th St.
New York, NY 10001
212/691-1910
www.leefilters.com

Lighting & Electronics, Inc.
Market St. Industrial Park
Wappingers Falls, NY 12590
914/297-1244
www.lpe.com

Lowel-Light Manufacturing
175 10th Ave.
New York, NY 10018
212/947-0950
www.lowel.com

LTM Corp. of America
1160 N. Las Palmas Ave.
Hollywood, CA 90038
213/460-6166
www.ltmlighting.com

Matthews Studio Equipment
2405 Empire Ave.
Burbank, CA 91504
818/843-6715
www.matthewsstudioequipmentinc.com

Mole-Richardson
937 N. Sycamore Ave.
Hollywood, CA 90038
213/851-0111
www.mole.com

Photo Research
3000 N. Hollywood Way
Burbank, CA 91505
213/849-6017
www.photoresearch.com

Rosco Laboratories
1135 N. Highland Ave.
Hollywood, CA 90038
213/462-2233
www.rosco.com

Rosco Laboratories
36 Bush Ave.
Port Chester, NY 10573
914/937-1300
www.rosco.com

Sanders Lighting Templates
5830 W. Patterson Ave.
Chicago, IL 60634-2680
312/736-9551
www.sanderspro.com

Stage Lighting Distributors
346 W. 44th St.
New York, NY 10036
212/489-1370
No Website

Stewart Filmscreen Corp.
1161 W. Sepulveda Blvd.
Torrance, CA 90502
213/326-1422
www.stewartfilm.com

Strand-Century
18111 S. Sante Fe Ave.
Rancho Dominguez, CA 90224
213/367-7500
www.strandlight.com

Sylvania Lighting Center
630 5th Ave., Suite 2670
New York, NY 10111
212/603-0700
No Website

Sylvania Lighting Center
800 Devon Ave.
Elk Grove Village, IL 60007
312/593-3400
No Website

Sylvania Lighting Center
6505 E. Gayhart St.
PO Box 2795
Los Angeles, CA 90051
213/726-1666
No Website

Tectronics
3100 McMillan Rd.
San Luis Obispo, CA 93401
805/544-3555
www.tectronics.com

Tiffen
90 Oser Ave.
Hauppauge, NY 11788
516/273-2500
www.tiffen.com

Ultimatte Corp.
18607 Topham St.
Reseda, CA 91335
818/993-8007
www.ultimatte.com

Ultra Light
7270 Bellaire Ave.
North Hollywood, CA 91605
818/765-2200
www.ulcs.com

Victor Duncan, Inc.
661 N. LaSalle St.
Chicago, IL 60610
312/943-7300
www.lightingdimensions.com

Victor Duncan, Inc.
6305 N. O'Connor, Suite 100
Irving, TX 75039
214/869-0200
www.lightingdimensions.com

Victor Duncan, Inc.
32380 Howard
Madison Heights, MI 48071
313/589-1900
www.lightingdimensions.com

Videotek
243 Shoemaker Road
Pottstown, PA 19464
800/800-5719
www.videotek.com

Visual Departures, Ltd.
1601 3rd Ave.
New York, NY 10128
212/534-1718
www.visualdepartures.com

Recommended Readings

Periodicals

Here is a list of publications that deal with up-to-date information about lighting techniques and equipment. Many are available without charge and others have an annual subscription rate. All are excellent sources for a broad spectrum of professional tips and techniques.

American Cinematographer
1782 North Orange Drive Hollywood, CA 90028
www.theasc.com

AV/Video Producer
25550 Hawthorne Blvd., Suite 314 Torrance, CA 90505
www.avvideo.com

Broadcast Engineering
295 Madison Ave. New York, NY 10017
www.broadcastengineering.com

Cinematographer
www.creativeplanet.com

Government Video
460 Park Avenue South, 9th Flr
New York, NY 10016
www.governmentvideo.com

Lighting Dimensions
PO Box 425 Mt. Morris, IL 61054-9907
www.lightingdimensions.com

Millimeter
12 E. 46th St. New York, NY 10017
www.millimeter.com

Strandlight
Rank Strand Ltd.
PO Box 51, Great West Rd.
Brentford, Middlesex TW8 9HR
United Kingdom
No Website

Theatre Crafts
33 E. Minor St. Emmaus, PA 18049
www.bluedolphin.com

TV Technology
5827 Columbia Pike
Third Floor
Falls Church, VA 22041
www.tv-technology.com

Videography
460 Park Ave. South, 9th Flr
New York, NY 10016
www.videography.com

Video News IC
Knowledge Industry Publications, Inc.
701 Westchester Ave.
White Plains, NY 10604
www.icommag.com

Video Systems
Box 12901
Overland Park, KS 66212
www.videosystems.primediabusiness.com

Index

About the Authors

Chuck Gloman

Growing up watching nightly old 1920's comedies with his father, Chuck Gloman was bitten by the film bug at an early age. Instead of critiquing films, he though it would be more fun to create them.

Enrolled in the film program in Pennsylvania State University, he created numerous student films that were later marketed on video. His Masters Thesis Film, a 1920's-style comedy short entitled "The Butler Did It," was sold to Home Box Office and Cinemax, where it enjoyed a nine-year run. After receiving a Bachelors Degree, he stayed on and was the first student in Penn State's history to complete a Masters Degree in Film/Theatre. While working toward his Masters, he taught intermediate and advanced film production. Upon graduation he joined the video world and created interactive videos for a community college. From there he worked with the US Armed Forces, Federal Express, and IBM and produced and directed over 50 interactive videodiscs. With the corporate training world beckoning, he shot and lit over 200 informational, corporate, and training tapes.

In the mid-1990's he created his own independent production company, No Splash Productions, and shot corporate training films and videos as well as television commercials. From there he worked at a local NBC affiliate and directed and lit over 600 television commercials.

Currently, he is an independent producer and director of photography, writes for several magazines and is looking forward to developing his own lighting instrument, the "Glo-light."

Tom LeTourneau

As Ted Baxter Was fond of saying, "It all began at a 5000-watt radio station in Fresno, California."

For Tom LeTourneau it began at a 1000-watt radio station in northern Wisconsin. And what does a radio announcer know about lighting? For one thing, he knows that when pranksters turn the lights out in the studio while you are reading a live newscast, you had better be prepared to tap dance or come up with some creative lighting.

His solution to that all-too-frequent lighting problem was to hold the copy against the glass face-plate of the VU meter so that the VU's small lamps acted as a backlight to the paper—and keep on reading. It took the puzzled pranksters several weeks to figure out how someone could read UPI wire copy in the dark. When they learned his secret they also learned a valuable lesson. No aspect of lighting is too small to be ignored, a fact LeTourneau has been espousing ever since. (They also learned how to remove the small lamps from a VU meter and to laugh at the sound of tap dancing.)

From those early days of solving lighting problems in radio and learning to read ahead of flaming scripts, LeTourneau moved on to television as an audio man, director, producer and lighting designer. After more than 25 years in the business, he has opened his own production company and provides a full range of production services for his commercial and industrial clients in Chicago. He also conducts lighting and directing seminars around the country.